COUNTRY
HOUSES
❧ OF BRITAIN & IRELAND ❧

COUNTRY HOUSES
OF BRITAIN & IRELAND

TOM QUINN

Photography by

PAUL RIDDLE

NEW HOLLAND

First published in 2005 by New Holland Publishers (UK) Ltd
London • Cape Town • Sydney • Auckland

www.newhollandpublishers.com

Garfield House, 86–88 Edgware Road, London W2 2EA, United Kingdom

80 McKenzie Street, Cape Town 8001, South Africa

14 Aquatic Drive, Frenchs Forest, NSW 2086, Australia

218 Lake Road, Northcote, Auckland, New Zealand

10 9 8 7 6 5 4 3 2 1

ISBN 1 84330 899 1

Publishing Manager: Jo Hemmings
Senior Editor: Kate Michell
Assistant Editors: Kate Parker, Rose Hudson
Design Concept: Alan Marshall
Designer: Ian Hughes, Mousemat Design
Cartographer: William Smuts
Indexer: Dorothy Frame
Production: Joan Woodroffe

Reproduction by Pica Digital Pte Ltd, Singapore
Printed and bound in Singapore by Kyodo Printing Co. (Singapore) Pte Ltd

Photographs appearing on the cover and prelim pages are as follows:
Front cover: Owlpen Manor, Gloucestershire, England.
Back cover: Blenheim Palace, Oxfordshire, England.
Front cover flap: Knebworth House, Hertfordshire, England
Opposite: The Palladian bridge in the grounds at Wilton House, Wiltshire,
England.
Page 6: Details from Syon House, London, England.
Page 7: Belvoir Castle, Leicestershire, England.

CONTENTS

INTRODUCTION

In Britain, the idea of the country house has always had enormous resonance. For centuries, important men built large houses in the rural areas of England and Wales, Scotland and Ireland, not necessarily as homes but as enduring embodiments of their status in the world. There are numerous examples of splendid houses built at great effort and expense but rarely lived in by their owners. Burghley House, constructed by Elizabeth I's closest adviser William Cecil (later Lord Burghley) near Stamford in Lincolnshire in the 16th century, is a fine example: Lincolnshire was the family's home county, but simply too far from London for frequent habitation, as Cecil knew when he commissioned the house. Even today, many of those who make their fortunes in the City or elsewhere feel the need at some stage to acquire a house away from the town, to retreat to some corner of the countryside and make it their own. Building – or, more usually nowadays, buying – a big house in the country is a way of saying, in more than one sense: 'I have arrived.'

A Man's House is his Castle

The earliest country houses that have survived are castles modified for domestic use, and early fortified manors. The latter are interesting as examples of transitional architecture: many of their features – towers, crenellations, arrow-slits – were already long out of date by the time they were built, but the idea that a house should be an impregnable fortress, and the styles associated with that idea, endured long after the need for genuine fortification had passed.

During the 18th and 19th centuries, visitors from all over Europe – and particularly from Russia – tried to copy at home the houses they saw in Britain, motivated by the civilized and civilizing spirit which the country house and, more importantly, the country-house way of life, seemed to embody: a way of existence which, for those at the centre of it, appeared the epitome of cultured life. With numerous servants to look after them, the guests at a country-house party could forget the practical necessities of everyday life and indulge their passion for luxurious living: outside for hunting, shooting and fishing; inside for food, drink, music and conversation. The longing for this way of life was best expressed even as it was dying: the mid-20th-century Evelyn Waugh novel *Brideshead Revisited* and poems like John Betjeman's 'Summoned by Bells' lament the passing of a way of life centred on and inextricable from the country house.

Conversely, there have been periods when the country-house ideal was deeply unfashionable. Alexander Pope, in his poem of 1717 'To Miss Blount on her leaving the Town after the Coronation', compares a young woman's life in London with her life in a country house:

She went, to plain-work and to purling brooks
Old-fashioned halls, dull aunts, and croaking rooks.
She went from Op'ra, park, assembly, play
To morning walks and prayers three hours a day.

Opposite: The Marble Hall, which dates from 1612 and is filled with purpose-made furniture, at Hatfield House in Hertfordshire is one of the most impressive rooms to be found in any of England's plentiful country houses.

Changing Trends

Reaction against the gloom of medieval houses – their tiny windows, rambling structure and small rooms – led to the great period of rebuilding in the 17th and 18th centuries, when the influence of Italian architects like Palladio revolutionized the ideal of the country house. Down came the medieval manors – which today we see, where they survive unaltered, as wonderfully picturesque – and up sprang houses with classical façades and clean, bright, high-ceilinged interiors designed by the brothers Robert and James Adam and others influenced by classical motifs.

Only rarely do we know anything about the architects or builders of medieval, Tudor and Elizabethan houses, but by the 18th century the leading architects were prominent members of society, and the services of the most fashionable were eagerly sought by aristocrats and wealthy merchants: among these coming men were, in addition to the Adam brothers, John Carr, George Dance the Elder and Younger, John Vanbrugh and many others.

By the later 18th century and into the early 19th, the taste for classical elegance had begun to wane, to be overtaken by a passion for what was seen as a more romantic, genuinely English style of architecture: thus emerged the Gothic Revival, which harked back to the principles that had underlain the design of the great medieval cathedrals. This shift in architectural taste coincided with the new enthusiasm in poetry, music and literature for the wild and ungovernable, the non-rational impulses that drove the Romantic movement. Among the best-known Gothic Revival architects was James Wyatt, who was called in to remodel, sometimes rebuild, many great houses. Whether he improved or damaged these houses is a question still open to debate.

Victorian architecture saw the romance of Gothic drift slowly into the heavy and overbearing, a style which is very unfashionable today. That period's architects are remembered better for their mass terraced housing than for grand gestures on the country-house scale.

Enduring Charm

This book includes wonderful houses from every period: great and sometimes quirky classical houses; rambling medieval manor houses; small, perfectly proportioned Jacobean and Georgian houses; and huge palatial constructions of the 18th and 19th centuries.

Despite the 18th- and 19th-century mania for rebuilding, some late medieval houses escaped modernization, thanks partly to the innate conservatism of their owners and partly, in some cases, to those owners' relative poverty and their distance from centres of fashion. But the great houses of England, Scotland, Wales and Ireland that survive today are monuments as much to the long-forgotten men and women who built them as to the wealthy individuals who commissioned the greatest architects, designers, painters, plasterers, woodcarvers and furniture-makers to do the work.

The great thing about the country house is its ability to endure, adapting to meet changing circumstances and changing interpretations. Just as castles and early manor houses were gradually modified to meet the demands of less war-like epochs, so in the 20th and 21st centuries increasing numbers of country-house owners realized that their properties could enjoy a new lease of life, a new period of prosperity, by opening

Opposite: The classical splendour of Holkham Hall transports the visitor to an Italian palazzo, but in reality Holkham was built as the private residence of rich country squires, the Cokes.

their doors to a wider public. The country-house weekends so beloved of the poet John Betjeman may largely be a thing of the past, but even in their heyday they were enjoyed only by the privileged few. Through the work of the National Trust, English Heritage and the Historic Houses Association everyone can now enjoy the pleasures of country-house visiting. Greater access over the past 50 or 60 years has also made us realize that Britain's country houses – including many that are still privately owned – are our greatest repository of art, whether it be painting, woodcarving, plasterwork, sculpture, furniture, clock-making or gardening.

Grand Survivors

It is said that Britain lost more than 98 per cent of all its art during the Reformation. The iconoclasts spared little as statues were smashed, paintings burned, and murals hacked away or covered up, and since almost all medieval art was religious the loss was grievous. But what we lost in ecclesiastical treasures we made up for with the rise of the country house and the national passion among the gentry and the aristocracy for collecting; a passion fuelled by the European travels of young and wealthy men on the Grand Tour.

If country houses last – and, despite the serious threats to their survival in the first half of the 20th century, many have lasted – so too, though less often, do the families who built them. A few examples will suffice to show the extraordinary devotion of individual families to particular houses: the Throckmortons have been at Coughton since 1409 and the earls of Wemyss have been at Stanway in Gloucestershire since at least the 14th century. Great landowning families like these once wielded enormous power both locally and nationally, and so the country house became an important political centre.

The power of the landowning class can be judged, for example, by the fact that the great period of enclosure at the end of the 18th century was pushed through Parliament by the very families who would benefit most from it. Enclosure – the transfer of millions of acres of common land into private ownership (with, it has to be said, little or no compensation for the poor who had hitherto relied on their commoners' rights for their livelihood) meant that the owners of great country houses could extend or adapt their parkland to suit their own purposes, diverting footpaths at will and even in a number of cases demolishing whole villages to improve the view from their drawing-room windows.

The great benefits enjoyed by country-house owners at the period of enclosure were matched only by the benefits they enjoyed at the Dissolution of the Monasteries over two centuries earlier, when Henry VIII put most of the church's huge holdings of land into the hands of his favourites. Within a few years, great houses appeared where once monasteries had been – hence the frequency of the word 'abbey' in country-house names. Though many monastic buildings were destroyed or allowed to fall into decay, some families reused the abbey buildings in a way that preserved their structure largely intact.

For many (though by no means all) country-house owners, the late 19th and early 20th centuries posed a new difficulty. For centuries they had relied on an endless supply of cheap servants from the local working population, but this supply began to dry up as factories began to offer better wages and conditions. After the First World War the 'servant problem', combined with increased taxes and the decline of the country house as a centre of political patronage, led eventually to a disastrous epidemic of demolitions, accelerating after the Second World War, in which hundreds of great houses were lost. During 1956, according to one estimate, an average of one country house a day was demolished in Britain. But even as these houses disappeared, the National Trust and other organizations were mobilizing to save what has come to be known as our built heritage. They have been singularly successful and now, wherever you live in Britain or Ireland, you will not be far from a country house of great beauty and historical interest. This book is a celebration of the best of those houses: some are already well known, others less so, but together they provide the modern visitor with a unique route into the living history of Britain.

South of England

From the ancient granite and stone manor houses of the rugged south-west to the warm elegance and beauty of brick-built Kentish houses such as Squerryes Court, the south of England is extraordinarily rich in great country houses from every period. There are vast, palatial houses, for example Burghley and Hatfield; smaller but no less perfect houses like Stanway in Gloucestershire – an estate owned by just two families in over 1000 years; and hidden gems such as Chastleton, an exquisite Jacobean house that time seems to have forgotten.

GODOLPHIN HOUSE

Godolphin is a splendid, largely Tudor and Stuart house, built originally for a family whose growing importance reflected their prominence in the tin-mining industry, a mainstay of the Cornish economy. Gradually, the family's wealth was transformed into political influence and the Godolphins, who lived in this beautiful granite house until the 18th century, became one of the most important of all Cornish families, serving successive monarchs in a number of posts. For example, towards the end of the 16th century, Sir Francis Godolphin was appointed governor of the Scilly Isles and Sidney Godolphin was Queen Anne's Lord Treasurer from 1702 to 1710.

Moving with the Times

Goldolphin House has changed considerably over the centuries. The original dwelling was built round two courtyards and dates from 1475. In about 1535, the house was given a new front, with two towers and a connecting curtain wall between them. The north range was later built on top of this wall, supported on loggias. By 1635, building work was largely complete, although there were later demolitions and minor alterations in the late 17th, 18th and 19th centuries.

By the early 18th century, especially after Sidney Godolphin's appointment as Lord Treasurer, the family were spending less time at their Cornish seat. Godolphin was created earl for his services to the Queen, and his son married the Duke of Marlborough's daughter. By the time this son inherited the title, the family's connections with Cornwall were tenuous, and in 1766, with the death of the second earl, the whole estate passed to a cousin and thence to the dukes of Leeds. By 1805, much of the early house, including the magnificent hall, had been demolished. What had become a farmhouse – albeit a rather splendid one – was finally sold by the Duke of Leeds in the 1920s.

Despite the destruction of so much of the house, what remains is fascinating. Today, when you face the front across the forecourt, you are looking at what was originally the

Opposite: *Godolphin House was built on the proceeds of tin mining, and has 15th-century origins.*

Below: *Light from a 17th-century mullioned window floods a bedroom of Godolphin House, which is gradually being restored to its former glory.*

Previous page: *Restrained elegance in the staircase at Firle Place in Sussex.*

north range, with its splendid colonnade of Tuscan columns and original mullioned 17th-century windows. The gateway, which was completed even earlier – in 1575 – leads into the courtyard where the east and west ranges also survive. A curious feature of the house is the undulating slate roof – a style found only in Devon and Cornwall.

The atmospheric interior has much to recommend it. There is a magnificent 16th-century chimneypiece in the Entrance Hall, and in the Dining Room massive beams and exquisite panelling evoke the earliest origins of the building. The King's Room has a beautiful overmantel (brought here from the Great Hall), made in 1610 to commemorate the marriage six years earlier between Sir William Godolphin and Thomasin Sidney. There is a pine floor in the north range dating back to 1630, almost certainly the oldest pine floor in the country.

Armour and Orchards

Fine furniture, pictures and tapestries can be found throughout the house. The highlight of the collection is undoubtedly the portrait by John Wootton of the Godolphin Arabian; this stallion, owned by Francis Godolphin, the second earl, was one of the most famous racehorses of all time and one of the three founding sires of the English Thoroughbred.

The beautiful Elizabethan stables still exist; today they are home to a collection of horse-drawn vehicles and a small collection of arms and armour, as well as a shop that sells a wide range of edible and medicinal herbs, local cheeses, unusual clothing and other items.

Outside there are orchards and gardens, including Cornwall's oldest formal garden, most of which dates to about 1500 but a third of which is two centuries older. There are carp ponds in the grounds, a reminder that these fish were a vital source of food in the Middle Ages. Woodlands, rich in bluebells in spring, complete the scene.

Although the house is privately owned, the 550-acre estate that surrounds it is owned by the National Trust. It includes Godolphin Hill, with its wonderful views, and many archaeological features, including Bronze Age enclosures and 19th-century mine buildings.

Right: The ornately carved doorway in the King's Room was made in 1610 to commemorate the wedding of Sir William Godolphin.

HARTLAND ABBEY

Hartland is a fascinating, entirely English amalgam of styles and periods. Originally built as an Augustinian abbey, it was transferred into private ownership by Henry VIII at the Dissolution of the Monasteries and has never been bought or sold in its long history. The particular glory of its setting, tucked away in a hidden valley – a seclusion which must have seemed ideal to those long-dead monks – has been recognized in its recent designation as a Site of Outstanding Natural Beauty, a haven of quiet rich in wildlife just a mile or so from the crashing waves of the Atlantic seaboard.

Monastic Heritage

The original monastic buildings at Hartland took more than a decade to complete and the abbey was consecrated in 1157. After almost four centuries of monastic seclusion, Hartland suffered the political upheavals of the Reformation and Henry VIII's greed. The monks were expelled and Hartland became a private dwelling – in fact, Hartland has the dubious distinction of being the last monastic house to be closed under Henry's edict.

William Abbott, a man glorying in the title of Sergeant of the King's Wine Cellar, was given the land and buildings at Hartland some time in the 1540s. One of his daughters, Prudence, inherited the property in 1583 and it passed into the Luttrell family on her marriage to Andrew Luttrell. At the beginning of the 18th century, the estate passed into the Orchard family, again through a daughter; a century later, in 1812, it passed through a third generation of the female line

Below: Gothic windows dominate the façade of Hartland Abbey, which was built in 1779 to replace the former abbey building.

into the Buck family. George Buck changed his name to Stucley (an old family name) on being made a baronet in 1859.

Eighteenth-century Influences

Today, the house looks very different from the abbey it once was, but much of the early fabric remains, a ghostly reminder of the great age of the building. Little work was done in the first two centuries following the suppression of the monastery other than simply making the main buildings more comfortable. The 18th century, the great age of rebuilding, saw the first major alterations to the house when the whole of the main body of the old building was reduced to the

height of the cloisters, the Chapel and Great Hall being completely demolished. Above the cloisters new rooms were built on two levels and the whole house was given a Gothic Revival façade.

The Victorian love of bay windows can be seen in the additions of the mid-19th century. The man behind the Victorian work was Sir George Stucley, who had a lively sense of his family's past: in the Drawing Room and Dining Room visitors can still see the murals he commissioned showing great historic events in which his ancestors played a part. The Regency style can be seen in the beautiful Library, and the house also contains one of Sir George Gilbert Scott's greatest

Below: Affection for the Gothic style can be seen in the interior of Hartland Abbey, too, although the rooms are still quite modest in size and decoration.

surviving works – the Alhambra Passage, with its beautiful vaulted and stencilled ceiling.

The Past Preserved

If you want a glimpse of one of the few remaining parts of the original abbey you will need to go into the cloisters, which are largely unchanged – even some of the doors here are original. Another way into the distant past is through the fascinating collection of early documents: rediscovered in the 1950s after being lost for centuries, they cover all aspects of the house and estate back to 1160.

In the abbey grounds, woodland walks became a feature in the 18th century. Early in the 20th century, the great Gertrude Jekyll came here and worked with Marion Lady Stucley to create the beautiful gardens we see today – gardens recovered after years of neglect, hidden under huge tangles of brambles and briars, including the Baronet's Bog Garden, the Camellia Garden and the Victorian Fernery. The Ladies' Walk leads down to four secret 18th-century walled gardens, one now used to grow vegetables.

Further afield the grounds lead to the rocky cove and the pounding sea. As you descend to the shore you are likely to encounter some of the wonderful birds and animals that populate the grounds, among them peacocks and bantams and, in the old deer park, donkeys and Black Welsh Mountain sheep.

Above: This vaulted, stencilled ceiling is one of the more impressive features of the Alhambra Corridor, designed by Sir Gilbert Scott in 1845.

Left: Arthurian murals, linenfold panels and a Jacobean revival fireplace in the drawing room are all part of Scott's interior design.

Right: *The Red Library, which is just one of seven libraries in the house, is richly decorated in heavily embossed wall-coverings and a gilded ceiling, again the work of J.G. Crace.*

and adapted over the centuries and that process continues to this day – the seventh marquess, for example, has added his own splendid murals throughout the west wing. In fact, though externally the house is clearly Elizabethan, internally little remains of the original decoration. The Thynnes always had enough money to follow current fashion, and during the 17th century those consulted included Sir Christopher Wren.

The most immediately striking thing about the Great Hall is its height – an impressive 35 feet. The ceiling is decorated with the arms of the Thynnes, while above the Minstrels' Gallery are the arms of the man who did most to promote John Thynne's career – Lord Protector Somerset. There have been several changes and additions to the panelling, which dates from different periods, as well as to the finish on walls and ceilings, the position of internal doorways, and lighting – records show that there were some very grand early gilt-wood chandeliers, now long gone.

Vast hunting scenes by John Wootton adorn the walls; the beautiful chimneypiece and the huge beams that hold up the roof are original. A painting by Jan Siberechts shows a view of Longleat in 1675. The antlers on either side of the State Drawing Gallery are those of prehistoric giant fallow deer (*Megaloceros*) and came from the family's Irish estate. The room also contains a 33-foot-long Tudor table, originally used to play shuffleboard.

A Book-Lover's Dream

The Red Library is one of seven libraries in the house – Longleat has a total of more than 40,000 books, including very early editions of Chaucer and works relating to the original building of the house. The Red Library also contains an evocative painting of the sisters of the Earl of Essex, the favourite of Elizabeth I who fell from favour and was executed in 1601. This library is also said to be haunted by a man in black about whom nothing is known.

The most famous ghost – still regularly seen – is Lady Louisa Carteret, wife of the second Viscount Weymouth, whose portrait

Right: Jeffry Wyatville's Grand Staircase, which was part of his remodelling of the entire house between 1806 and 1813, replaced a staircase designed by Sir Christopher Wren.

hangs in the Lower Dining Room (she haunts the corridor upstairs known as the Grey Lady's Walk).

The Lower Dining Room is filled with 16th- and 17th-century family portraits hanging below an elaborate Victorian ceiling (a copy of one found in the Doge's Palace in Venice). One of the portraits is by a woman, Mary Beale, who became famous despite the contemporary prejudice against well-born women doing any kind of work, let alone portraiture of the great. There is also a painting here of the John Thynne who built Longleat. The room contains, in addition, magnificent 18th-century Sèvres porcelain and two unusual ebony side-chairs inlaid with ivory.

State Rooms

The State Dining Room, designed to entertain royalty and other dignitaries, contains 17th-century embossed leather wall coverings from Spain, classical pictures by a follower of Titian and a portrait of Isabella Rich, the wife of Sir James Thynne, who was banned from court by Charles I for dancing naked (it is said) on London Bridge! In the centre of the dining table is a 4-foot-high Meissen Temple of Minerva.

The 90-foot Saloon was originally the long gallery, a feature without which no Elizabethan house was complete. The ceiling, by the Victorian designer J.G. Crace who did a great deal of redecorating work at Longleat, is a copy of one in the Palazzo Massimo in Rome, while the gigantic 19th-century marble fireplace is a copy of one in the Doge's Palace in Venice. The gallery is filled with Italian and French 18th-century furniture and there are 17th-century Flemish tapestries on the walls.

The State Drawing Room was redesigned by Crace to house a collection of Italian paintings, including Titian's *Rest on the Flight into Egypt* and pictures by Tintoretto and Granacci.

Art and Artefacts

A display of largely Victorian clothing and Sèvres porcelain can be seen in the Robes Corridor. The Grand Staircase was added in the early 19th century by Jeffry Wyatville, replacing one by Christopher Wren. On the walls are family portraits, hunting scenes and a family tree going back to 1215. Unusually, there is a memorial to the Longleat librarian, George Harbin. There is also a portrait of Simon Jude Cole, the steward of the Longleat Estates (1742–79).

In the west wing are the present marquess's own murals. Having studied art, he moved into this part of the house in 1953 and completed the first mural in 1964. He describes the series as a 'glimpse into my psyche' and explains that the pictures might best be summed up as 'cocoons, fantasies and therapies'.

A whistlestop tour of Longleat can hardly take account of the vast array of furniture, mostly Italian and French, that fills the house, nor of the sense that this is essentially an early 19th-century house behind an Elizabethan façade – modernization was a passion of the second marquess, who employed Wyatville to undertake substantial alterations in the house as well as to add a new stable block and orangery. Work continued apace under the watchful eye of the fourth marquess, who commissioned J.G. Crace in the 1870s to create the elaborate Italian Renaissance-style ceilings and other interiors we see today.

On Safari

Outside, the grounds cover an impressive 1,100 acres of parkland, landscaped first by the ubiquitous Lancelot 'Capability' Brown and later by Humphry Repton, and 8,000 further acres of woodland, farmland and lakes. Most famously, of course, Longleat's Safari Park is here – the first of its kind outside Africa, created by the sixth marquess in 1966. Longleat was also the first stately home to open its doors to the public, in 1949.

Continuing the traditions of his ancestors, the present marquess has made major changes to the gardens; among his innovations has been a series of mazes, including the World's Longest Hedge Maze (1975), the Love Labyrinth (1993), the Sun Maze (1996) and the Lunar Labyrinth (1996).

WILTON HOUSE

Built on the site of a Benedictine abbey, Wilton House was given by Henry VIII to William Herbert in 1542, and the Herberts have been here ever since. The current owner, William Herbert, is the 18th Earl of Pembroke and 15th Earl of Montgomery. The house has been remodelled a number of times – particularly at the beginning of the 19th century – but 17th-century elements also survive, including what is generally agreed to be the finest mid-17th-century interior in the country: the Double Cube Room.

Below: *Wilton House is a sight for sore eyes, with interiors by Inigo Jones and James Wyatt.*

The Double Cube Room

This magnificently ornate gilded room, 60 feet long, 30 feet wide and 30 feet high, was designed by the earliest and greatest of English classical architects, Inigo Jones, and his nephew John Webb, in a baroque version of the classical style. It forms part of the south wing of the house, the earliest extant example of English Palladian architecture, completed between 1647 and 1653 and left relatively

unscathed by later remodelling. This part of the house is almost certainly the only surviving example of a domestic building by Inigo Jones.

The Double Cube Room, originally called the State Room and one of the most famous rooms in any house in the country, has been much imitated and is used as a gallery for the Wilton Van Dyck collection. The Van Dyck pictures, brought to Wilton from the Pembrokes' London house in the 1650s, include a family portrait that measures an extraordinary 17 feet by 11 feet – the biggest picture the artist ever painted.

Wyatt, Chippendale and Palladio

Various parts of the house were redesigned in the early 1800s by James Wyatt – the Gothic Hall, for example, and the cloisters, which were designed as far as possible to imitate the medieval style and completed in 1815. The

Left: A detail of a carved stone angel overlooks the fine landscaped gardens of Wilton House.

Below: The south front of the house looks out to the lake and is the earliest example of English Palladian architecture. It was designed by Inigo Jones and his pupil John Webb in 1648.

Large Smoking Room is famous not so much for its design as for the furniture it contains: commissioned for this very room and made by

Below: Penshurst Place evolved from the Great Hall, seen here in the centre left of the picture, to the large house we see today. The wonderfully restored gardens are true to their original design thanks to the preservation of Penshurst's garden records as far back as the 14th century.

IGHTHAM MOTE

Ightham Mote is one of those rare houses that always brings a gasp of astonishment from visitors seeing it for the first time: everything seems to conspire to make it special. Lying in a sunken valley surrounded by a moat, it was never a grand house or a great fortified stronghold of the sort that survives in some numbers across Kent and Sussex. Rather, Ightham is simply a small manor house, and an extremely early one at that. It dates from as early as 1330, and although various owners left their mark on it, the essential medieval character of this multi-faceted house remains. Because of its delicate, fragile beauty the house has been extensively conserved by the National Trust.

Defended by Water

Ightham's ragstone lower walls rise sheer from its deep moat, but then the stone ends and the beautiful half-timbered second storey begins. Here and there the timber projects out over the moat, reminding us of the jettied style of building once common right across the south of England, including London, where overhanging upper storeys would often almost meet above the narrow city streets.

Right: *A Saracen's head – the Selby family crest – has been carved into the newel post of Ightham Mote's Jacobean staircase.*

To reach the house you cross a small stone bridge – one of three – over the moat. The moat itself is fed by a stream which prevents it becoming stagnant. A curiosity of the entrance is the small slit – or 'squint', as it is more properly known – to the side of the gate where a letter could be delivered without the messenger being admitted to the house.

Of Chaucer's Time

We do not know who built Ightham, but by 1360 it was owned by a contemporary of Geoffrey Chaucer, Sir Thomas Cawne, who fought at Crécy. His monument can be seen today in full armour in Ightham church. Cawne's son Robert inherited the house in 1374, and he would still recognize the building he owned today. Not only the moat, but the Great Hall with its 14th-century roof, the Chapel, the Crypt and two family rooms or solars have all survived.

Most 14th-century houses and churches would have been untidy, even ramshackle by today's standards, with extra rooms and outbuildings added on almost randomly, often leaning against the main buildings. This would have been true at Ightham, where archaeological evidence suggests that wooden buildings were erected in the present courtyard; none survive today, although there are timber-framed buildings outside the moat. The courtyard was almost

Opposite: The mid-18th-century half-timbered cottages at Ightham Mote are part of one of the least altered, early country houses in England.

Below: The Great Hall at Ightham Mote would have originally been heated by a large central hearth, but its great size meant that keeping it warm and dry was always a struggle.

certainly not enclosed for the first century or so of the house's life, but by the end of the 15th century the tower gatehouse and fourth side of the courtyard had been added.

Ightham's Progress

Though it never had pretensions to grandeur, Ightham did undergo some alterations in the hands of the Tudor courtier Sir Richard Clement, who bought it for £400 in 1521. Clement added the Long Gallery (later to become the New Chapel) on the first floor, and the carved timber bargeboards in the courtyard. These bargeboards are decorated with the Tudor rose, pomegranates (the symbol of Granada, from where Henry VIII's first wife Catherine came) and the French *fleur de lis*. The Tudor rose and motifs are repeated in the five stained-glass windows of the Great Hall,

which originally would probably have been only small unglazed openings closed with wooden shutters.

The gatehouse leads into the courtyard, directly across from which is the Great Hall. Here the family would have eaten on a raised dais with servants and other retainers seated at long tables below them. Like other halls in houses of this type, heating would have been provided by a central hearth, from which the smoke would have simply drifted up and out through the roof. It would have been very dark and very draughty.

At one end of the hall a door leads to the beautiful Jacobean staircase commissioned by Sir William Selby (still retaining its carved Saracen's head – the family crest), who inherited the house from his uncle in 1611 and whose family were to remain at Ightham until the mid-19th century. The

48

A Fine Art Collection

By the early 18th century, the Warde family were living here. After John Warde's death in 1746, his son inherited the house and added greatly to the collection of paintings: most of the art he brought here remains, including work by 17th-century Dutch and Italian masters, as well as his acquisitions of furniture and porcelain.

The first room the visitor sees is the Hall, where above the fireplace hangs a painting of one Patience Warde, a family ancestor who became Lord Mayor of London. There is also, in the Dining Room, a splendid portrait of John Warde and his wife.

The staircase has beautiful family portraits by an anonymous 17th-century artist and there are early 18th-century Soho tapestries on the walls of the appropriately named Tapestry Room. Next comes the Wolfe Room, where items associated with

General Wolfe, hero of the battle for Quebec in 1759 and a family friend of the Wardes, can be seen.

The Drawing Room has a beautiful 18th-century plaster ceiling and contains Dutch 17th-century paintings and English gilt-framed mirrors; the Dining Room has early 18th-century walnut chairs, family portraits – including a magnificent painting by George Stubbs showing John Warde's son holding an Arab racehorse – and an original 17th-century fireplace.

In the Picture Gallery, among other fine works, are a portrait by Van Dyck and a Rubens portrait of Philip II of Spain.

The gardens are particularly attractive in spring, with great carpets of daffodils and bluebells; throughout the summer the herbaceous borders and old roses bloom continuously. The original plans still exist for the garden as it was designed in 1709.

Opposite: The rich classical interior of Squerryes Court.

Below: Formal gardens give way to herbaceous borders.

SYON HOUSE

The most extraordinary thing about Syon House, which is now surrounded by suburban London, is that behind the house and running down to the River Thames are meadows unchanged since the country all about was marshland and farmland. The monks who lived in the monastery that stood here before the present house was built would still recognize this landscape today.

Opposite: Entering Syon House is, at first, like entering a calm oasis thanks to the serene nature of the Great Hall, with its marble floor and grand Romanesque sculptures.

Below: The stark simplicity of the façade of Syon House belies the elaborate Adam interiors within.

A Family Home

The Percy family, dukes of Northumberland, have lived at Syon House since Tudor times when, like so many great families, they benefited from Henry VIII's falling out with the Pope and his appropriation of church buildings and funds. The present square-built house was largely remodelled in the 18th century, but contains a much earlier core.

Syon's great claim to fame today is that it has some of the very best of Robert Adam's characteristic interiors – he worked here in the 1760s – along with beautiful Georgian furniture and pictures. Externally the house has a curious castle-like appearance, with its corner towers and crenellations.

Political Players

The dukes of Northumberland (the earldom was created in 1377, the dukedom in 1766) were always at the centre of English political life, which explains why a number of family members were beheaded and why over the years many of the great and the good have stayed at the house: King Charles I came here, as did Princess Victoria before she became queen – the bedroom in which she stayed is open to visitors.

On its way to burial, Thomas Cromwell's coffin was left at Syon overnight, and in the morning the family's dogs were found to have knocked the lid off and feasted on the remains. This was said to be retribution for Cromwell's part, as Henry VIII's chief

Right: The magnificent Adam rooms at Syon House are among Adam's least-altered interiors anywhere in Britain. The State Dining Room is one of the most elegant rooms in the house.

Below: The gardens at Syon House, parts of which are private, run down to the River Thames.

adviser, in the destruction of the old abbey.

Syon House still has a little over 200 acres of parkland, 40 acres of which are garden, and from here there are lovely views in summer across the River Thames to Kew Gardens. There is a magnificent early 19th-century conservatory that, along with the state apartments (designed by Adam) and neo-classical Great Hall, can be hired for weddings and corporate events.

HAM HOUSE

It seems odd that London should have one of the best country houses in Britain, but of course it does so only because, over the centuries, the capital has crept out to embrace what were once small, isolated villages. At least one village, though surrounded now by suburban housing, still retains both its village character and a great country house: Ham.

A Riverside Residence

Sited a few hundred yards from the Thames and just half a mile or so from the busy streets of Richmond in one direction and Kingston in the other, Ham is actually on the edge of Petersham village and meadows. Despite developers' attempts at encroachment, the riverside meadows still graze herds of cattle in summer and the road winds awkwardly among the 18th-century houses of what is still recognizably a village. A narrow lane leads down to Ham House through fields grazed by horses and punctuated by small woods: a stretch of countryside that must look pretty much as it did when Ham House was built in the early 17th century.

Finished in 1610 for James I's knight marshal Sir Thomas Vavasour and then enlarged in the 1670s, Ham reminds us that wealthy Londoners always built their country retreats by the river since travel by water was so much easier than travel by unmade roads – particularly in winter, when the land routes were often impassable.

Opposite: Unchanged for almost 350 years, the Great Staircase at Ham House has elaborate carved and pierced panels for a balustrade.

Below: The garden at Ham House is not only famous for its lavender parterres, but also boasts a wonderful hornbeam tunnel.

Sir Thomas lived at Ham only until 1620, at which time the house passed to the earls of Holderness and then in 1626 to William Murray. Murray has the dubious distinction of having been Charles I's whipping boy. Heirs to the throne were far too important to be punished for their own misdeeds, so a boy of the same age was appointed to accompany the prince and take whatever punishment was meted out for the young royal's misdemeanours. Murray commissioned the Great Staircase, as well as the Great Dining Room, North Drawing Room and Long Gallery, and many of the pictures he hung in the house are still there today.

Lawmakers

Ham has been described as unique in Europe because a glimpse into the house is a glimpse not only into the architectural past but also the human past; into the social history of the aristocratic families who ran the country.

When William Murray died in 1665, the house passed to his daughter Elizabeth, who became Countess of Dysart. She married Lionel Tollemache in 1648, and when he died in 1669 she married the Duke of Lauderdale. Lauderdale redecorated much of the house and added furniture and fittings felt to be in keeping with his position as one of Charles II's most powerful ministers.

Lauderdale was Secretary of State for Scotland, and the work he and his wife carried out on the house survives to the present. The duchess was remarkable in many ways, not least because she refused to accept confinement to the usual domestic female role (although she gave birth to 11 children) and succeeded in exercising substantial political influence. Her ghost is said to the haunt the house.

Below: Extravagant gold leaf covers the ceiling of the Long Gallery, while two fireplaces sit opposite windows overlooking the gardens.

disgraced Walter Ralegh lost Sherborne Castle: see pages 22–4.) The work of the great miniaturist Nicholas Hilliard is also represented here in the Ermine Portrait of Elizabeth. Here she gazes out of the picture stern and aloof, watched by the small ferret-like ermine, a symbol of chastity, which rests its paws on her forearm.

To Be a Queen

It was while walking in the grounds here at Hatfield that Elizabeth heard that she was to be crowned queen following the death of her sister Mary. As a child, Elizabeth lived in the Old Palace of Hatfield, which was built in 1485. One wing of this medieval house survives in the grounds of the Jacobean house.

There are 3 miles of marked trails in and around the 5,000-acre estate, and the present Lady Salisbury has spent more than 30 years restoring the original 17th-century gardens, most of which disappeared in the 18th-century enthusiasm for Capability Brown and his followers. The original gardens were laid out by the great gardener and plant collector John Tradescant the Elder, whose family portraits now form a central part of the Ashmolean Museum in Oxford.

Today, the main points of interest for visitors to Hatfield are the state rooms where the great portraits and tapestries are to be found, but fascinating details can be found all over the house – not least, for example, on the great staircase, where the delicate carving pays tribute to the extraordinary skills of long-forgotten Jacobean craftsmen.

KNEBWORTH HOUSE

*Originally a red-brick Tudor manor house, Knebworth was swept up in the Victorian
passion for all things Gothic and rebuilt in 1843 in the style we see today – with
gargoyles, turrets and griffins; but the core of the house, in which the Lytton family
has lived for more than five centuries, retains a great deal of the Tudor original. The
house was the brainchild of the Victorian novelist Edward Bulwer Lytton. Charles
Dickens, the architect Edwin Lutyens and Winston Churchill were all visitors. In fact,
Lutyens married into the family and redesigned some of the Knebworth interiors, and
the great horticulturalist Gertrude Jekyll designed the herb garden.*

Gothic Glories

Sir Robert Lytton bought Knebworth in 1490 for £800. He transformed what had been a simple gatehouse into a quadrangle house which remained largely unaltered until 1810, when Mrs Elizabeth Bulwer Lytton demolished three sides of the house and buried the exterior of the remaining side under white stucco. It was at this time – around 1810 – that the windows were given a Gothic makeover and eight towers were added, together with battlements and a porch.

Elizabeth's son, the novelist Sir Edward Bulwer Lytton, no doubt fired by his mother's enthusiasm, continued her work. He employed the architect and designer H.E. Kendall to add yet more turrets, towers and gargoyles. By 1880, the Lyttons had been elevated to the peerage, and Edward Robert Bulwer Lytton, first Earl of Lytton, added another storey to the house. Admittedly, he needed more space for his family and household, having returned from his posting as Viceroy of India with five children. The Lutyens changes to the house were made after Victor, the second earl, came to live at Knebworth in 1908.

Arts and Crafts

Lutyens designed the Entrance Hall, which is the first area the visitor will see. It has two splendid wooden statues of Diana (the huntress) and Ceres (goddess of plenty), and wonderfully antique-looking panelling, as well as two curious high-backed chairs dating from the early 18th century. To the right of the Entrance Hall is the Picture Gallery with its 17th- and 18th-century family portraits.

The Banqueting Hall retains its late 16th-century ceiling and Tudor oak screen, together with pine panelling long thought to be the work of one of Inigo Jones's assistants, John Webb, but now thought more likely to be by William Talman. There is a portrait of Sir Robert Lytton, who built the original house, and a very fine portrait by Marcus Gheeraerts of Anne St John, cousin of Elizabeth I and wife of Sir Rowland Lytton.

The Dining Parlour has a Lutyens-designed fireplace and a dozen mid-19th-century applewood chairs. The Venetian glass bears the Lytton coat of arms and was

Previous page: Knebworth's picture gallery is hung with 17th- and 18th-century Lytton family portraits.

Right: Arms and armour give the staircase hall a rich, medieval feel.

made when Edward Robert Bulwer Lytton became Viceroy of India. There are family portraits by the Restoration court painter Sir Peter Lely, and by Samuel van Hoogstraten. One of the rarest objects in the house is to be found in the Library: a small crucifix owned by Mary, Queen of Scots and given to a lady in waiting just before her execution.

There is a collection of arms and armour on the staircase, as well as a large and decidedly romantic portrait of Edward Bulwer Lytton. Other subjects of portraits on the staircase include the great beauty Pamela, Countess of Lytton, and Neville, the third earl, who became a painter and lived in Paris; he did not inherit Knebworth, his brother Victor leaving the house instead to his daughter Hermione.

Ancestors Celebrated

The State Drawing Room is an excellent unaltered example of high Gothic Revival. There is a stained-glass portrait of Henry VII and on the ceiling are 44 panels representing the arms of the family's various ancestors. The fireplace here is a masterpiece of Gothic tracery and niches.

Other highlights in this splendid country house include the wonderful and vast collection of children's furniture, toys and books in the Hampden Room, and the Queen Elizabeth Room.

The garden is mainly Edwardian in its structure and layout, designed by Sir Edwin Lutyens between 1908 and 1911, but superimposed on Sir Edward Bulwer Lytton's elaborate Victorian design.

Below: Knebworth House has been altered so many times over the centuries, lastly during the height of the Victorian craze for the Gothic, that it now resembles a fantasy house: all turrets, cupolas and griffins.

AUDLEY END

A large house by almost any standards, Audley End was once three times its current size. It was completed in 1614 during the reign of James I by Thomas Howard, first Earl of Suffolk – largely, it is said, to impress the King, who stayed here many times. When first built, at a reputed cost of £200,000, Audley End was the biggest house in England, a palace in all but name.

Opposite: Typically Jacobean, the surviving exterior of Audley End has remained unaltered since it was completed in 1614 by the first Earl of Suffolk, although it is now a third of its original size.

Below: The chapel is a monumental example of the Gothic Revival style.

Howard's Legacy

Like so many English country houses, Audley End was built on the site of a monastic foundation, in this case, Walden Abbey – of which little remains other than a fishpond. The abbey was given to Thomas Howard, the grandfather of the man who built the house we see today, in the 1530s.

Stylistically, the house is, from the outside at least, typically Jacobean and apparently unchanged, but the interior has been significantly altered as various owners – including later generations of Howards – left

their mark. In 1668, Charles II bought Audley End (reputedly for £50,000) from the Howards, who had fallen on hard times, so that he would have somewhere to stay when he indulged his passion for horseracing at nearby Newmarket. However, by 1700 it was back in the hands of the Howard family, with whom it remained until the 20th century when, in 1948, it was sold to the government before being passed to the current owners, English Heritage.

The early 18th century saw the first period of demolition when, in 1701, the

Opposite: The moated Tudor mansion of Kentwell Hall is delightfully picturesque.

Below: The Great Hall, first occupied in the mid-16th century, was restored in the 19th century by Thomas Hopper and more recently refurbished with a touch of humour by its current owners.

and the cedar lawn is overlooked by giant cedars planted early in the 19th century.

The Moat House (a separate service building) has a central half-timbered section that was built in the 1470s; it is a rare survivor and still retains its bakehouse, dairy and brewhouse, with solar above. The solar has a squint – a narrow opening – through which the mistress of the house could keep an eye on those working below. The Moat House has been decorated by the present owners in a vaguely 15th-century style and wear and tear by visitors has made the decorative scheme remarkably authentic.

The Walled Garden, with its lawns and ancient fruit trees, is at least as old as the house itself. The current owners have created a new entrance-gate screen with two ogee-shaped, lead-topped Octagon Gatehouses (reflecting the twin towers of the house) and have established from scratch a Home Farm with a number of timber-framed and brick traditional farm buildings which house rare breeds of farm animal.

EUSTON HALL

At the time the Domesday Book was compiled, Euston Hall was a remote manor house deep in Suffolk and the property of the abbots of Bury St Edmunds. The medieval house still existed in Elizabethan times, records showing that Elizabeth I stayed there on one of her progresses around the country. At the end of the 16th century, the Rookwood family owned the house which, even then, must have seemed ancient.

Below: There was a manor house on this site at the time of the Domesday Book. However, today's Euston Hall dates back to the mid-17th century.

French Fashion

By the mid-1600s the estate had fallen on hard times and the house was dilapidated. It was then bought by Secretary of State Henry Bennet, Earl of Arlington. Bennet immediately decided to demolish the old house and build a grand new one in the French style – all things French being much in fashion after Charles II's return from his long exile in France.

The new house was square-built round a courtyard with pavilions at each corner. Bennet's daughter and son-in-law, the Duke of Grafton, inherited the house in 1685, but

it was their son who decided on the next major transformation, which took place in the 1750s. The Graftons employed Matthew Brettingham, who also served the Earl of Leicester as clerk of the works at Holkham Hall (see pages 81–4), to carry out the work, which included replacing the domes with low pyramid roofs and refacing parts of the house.

Tragedy Strikes

Thereafter, the house remained unaltered until tragedy struck in 1902, when much of the mid-18th-century work was lost in a fire that destroyed the south and west wings. The house was rebuilt in 1905, but the costs of maintaining it led the 10th Duke of Grafton to demolish most of the west wing and all the south wing in 1952. However, despite the destruction, much remains of interest in the surviving portions of the house.

Among the highlights of any visit are the 17th-century paintings of the court of Charles II by van Dyck and Lely, together with 'Mares and Foals', one of George Stubbs's finest works. There is also a good picture of the hall as it was in 1710. The staircase has a most unusual painting of King Charles II at a ball held in Holland on the night before he returned to England to become king. Charles's embroidered nightcase is also here.

The Outer Hall contains Lord Nelson's telescope and a barometer designed by Admiral Robert Fitzroy, the grandson of the fourth duke. Fitzroy commanded *The Beagle* during Darwin's epoch-making voyage. His name now replaces Finisterre in the shipping forecast.

Kent's Folly

There is a splendid temple in the grounds – an octagonal folly said to be the last

Below: This fine folly was the work of the architect and landscape gardener William Kent, who promoted the Palladian style of architecture in England.

completed work of William Kent (dated 1746) – and the beautiful Church of St Genevieve is a very rare example of a 17th-century church virtually unaltered since it was built.

During the period just after 1666, when the country's resources (raised through a special Coal Tax and other schemes) were going into rebuilding the dozens of London churches destroyed in the Great Fire, only four country churches were built, and St Genevieve's is one of them. The little-known architect E.M. Wilbraham completed the work, but Sir Christopher Wren is said to

have been consulted. There is some fine woodcarving by the great Grinling Gibbons.

One of the curiosities of Euston is that the Pleasure Gardens were laid out by the diarist John Evelyn, a contemporary of Samuel Pepys, who was a regular visitor to the house and by all accounts an expert on trees. He diverted the river into the Basin, which was later enlarged as the Broadwater by Capability Brown in the 1770s. The present watermill was designed by William Kent in 1731 to resemble a church, and was restored by the 11th Duke of Grafton as his millennium project.

Below: *The unpretentious Dining Room is where the Grafton family portraits can be found.*

SOMERLEYTON HALL

There was almost certainly a grand house at Somerleyton in late Saxon or early Norman times, but that timber structure was replaced by a stone house in about 1240. At that time it was owned by the Norman Fitzosberts. By the 14th century, the house had passed through a daughter to the Jernegan family, who owned it until 1604, when it was bought by John Wentworth. He demolished the old house and created the beautiful Jacobean house that was to last until the extremely wealthy entrepreneur and politician Sir Samuel Morton Peto transformed the house in the 1840s. Peto's passion for rebuilding was extraordinary by any standards: he applied it not only to the house, but also to the garden, the local church and even the estate cottages.

Below: *The impressive façade of Somerleyton Hall was paid for by the Victorian railway magnate Sir Morton Peto.*

Right: *The main entrance leads the visitor into a foyer dominated by a stained-glass dome.*

Only the Very Best

For the house, the finest craftsmen were employed using only the very best materials; pictures were commissioned from the most acclaimed artists of the day to hang in specific places. Peto was one of the last in a long tradition of hugely rich estate owners creating vast memorials to their own taste and judgement.

John Thomas, a well-known sculptor who also worked as an architect, was employed to design the new house. He was a protégé of Prince Albert and of Sir Charles Barry, architect of the new Palace of Westminster. Almost nothing of the Jacobean house was left after Thomas had completed his work, but the new house embodies all the virtues and some of the vices of that exuberant mid-Victorian period.

The front of the house is seen between the two wings that flank the courtyard. Across this courtyard and connecting the two wings is a carved stone screen designed in the French Renaissance style. One gable end of the wings still has the Dutch gables of the original Jacobean Hall – one of the few areas where the old house is still visible.

A magnificent Italian campanile gives wonderful views of the sea, and the courtyard has a clock designed by the renowned clock-maker Vulliamy. In the winter garden Peto commissioned Sir Joseph Paxton, architect of the Crystal Palace, to build a sort of miniature Crystal Palace at Somerleyton – sadly destroyed just after the Great War.

From Carriages to Carpets

However, by the early 1860s Peto was in deep financial trouble and had to sell the property to pay off his vast debts, estimated at £4 million. In 1863, the estate was bought by another self-made man: the carpet-maker Sir Francis Crossley of Halifax, great-grandfather of the present Lord Somerleyton.

Crossley had been something of an anti-establishment radical in his youth, but in the year he bought Somerleyton he became part of the establishment when he accepted a baronetcy in 1863. Sir Francis's son Sir Savile was elevated to the peerage in 1916 as Baron Somerleyton. The present Lord Somerleyton, the third baron, inherited the title in 1959.

Salvaged Treasures

The house itself contains much of interest. The Oak Room has 17th-century panelling and early carved doorcases incorporating sunflower and acanthus leaves; both the panelling and the doorcase carvings were salvaged from the Jacobean house. The carving on the chimneypiece – a mass of extraordinarily lifelike grapes, roses, cockerels and pomegranates – is said to be by Grinling Gibbons. On the north wall hangs a late 17th-century silver and gilt mirror, made originally for the Doge's Palace in Venice.

The Library, now used as a sitting room, was originally the banqueting hall. It has an unusual fireplace made in 1920 which bears the inscription 'Live to learn, Learn to live'. In the Dining Room there is a wonderful picture of Rembrandt with his wife Saskia by Rembrandt's pupil Ferdinand Bol. There are also two pictures by the 19th-century painter Clarkson Stanfield: 'The Siege of San Sebastian', showing Wellington in action in 1813, and 'HMS *Victory* Being Towed into Gibraltar Seven Days after the Battle of Trafalgar'. 'An Academy by Lamplight' by Joseph Wright of Derby, that great artist of the emerging industrial revolution, hangs above the sideboard.

The Staircase Hall, which has windows decorated with the coats of arms of the families that have held the Somerleyton estate since 1240, is filled with Crossley family portraits as well as the robes worn by the late Lord and Lady Somerleyton at the coronations of King George VI and the present Queen.

The Entrance Hall has stained glass windows in its dome and a centrepiece marble statue (by Sir Joseph Durham) of Sir Savile Crossley as a boy holding a spade in one hand and seashells in the other. The dolls' house is actually a model of the

Below: Also in the dark foyer, the visitor is greeted by two huge stuffed bears and a sculpture of a young Crossley.

Jacobean Somerleyton Hall.

In the Ballroom, mirrors reflect the carved figures – said to be the spirits of art and science – on fireplaces that face each other across the room. The passageway between the Ballroom and the Staircase Hall has a splendid picture of 'A Buck and Fawns' by Sir Edwin Landseer, Queen Victoria's favourite painter. Here, too, are an 18th-century Flemish tapestry and a collection of Crossley memorabilia, including a telegram telling Savile that his son had been wounded in the First World War.

The Conference Room, which was once the Billiard Room, has a splendid clock by Vulliamy and a series of watercolours showing how the house has changed over the years.

Acres to Explore

Outside there are 12 acres of gardens to explore. In spring the rhododendrons and azaleas blaze with colour. There is a magnificent equatorial sundial in the formal garden, while the clock in the stable tower was a model made for what was to become Big Ben – Vulliamy, the maker, found that his design was rejected on the grounds of cost so the model was bought by Morton Peto and erected here at Somerleyton.

The Walled Garden, formerly the kitchen garden, still has a range of glasshouses by Sir Joseph Paxton.

There is also a wonderful yew hedge maze that was planted in 1846, along with other original Victorian elements.

Right: An Italianate tower, one of the many additions to the original Jacobean house by Peto and his architect John Thomas, sits beside the main entrance to Somerleyton Hall.

HOLKHAM HALL

Many of the great country houses of Britain and Ireland are closely related to one another through the power relationships and fluctuating histories of the families who built and lived in them. The Cecils of Hatfield helped James I remove Walter Ralegh from Sherborne, the house he was given by Elizabeth I; Sir Edward Coke, whose family now own Holkham, was chief prosecutor of England in the time of James I and presented the case against Ralegh that led to his loss of Sherborne.

Modest, then Magnificent

Sir Edward Coke would not recognize Holkham today. The 25,000-acre estate surrounds a vast Palladian house completely unlike the relatively modest Elizabethan dwelling known as Hill Hall that Coke bought in 1609. It was almost a century later that Thomas Coke, first Earl of Leicester, decided to rebuild, hiring Matthew Brettingham as his clerk of works. The family was by that time enormously wealthy, and the earl had returned from a six-year tour of Europe during which he had met Lord Burlington (who was to build Chiswick House) and his architect William Kent. Coke was fired with enthusiasm for the newly fashionable Palladian style; he also needed somewhere to house the vast quantity of art books, manuscripts, drawings, paintings, tapestries and statuary he had collected during his years in Europe. Holkham Hall was the result.

The size of the house can be judged by the length of time it took to build: more

Below: Vast and palatial Holkham Hall stands majestically among its 3,000 acres of grounds.

than 30 years in all. When Thomas died in 1759 the estate passed to his widow.

The Origins of the Bowler Hat

One of the fascinating historical details about Holkham is that the bowler hat, so often thought of as exclusively City wear, was invented here. It was originally known as the Billycock and was designed to protect Coke's keepers' heads should they be attacked by poachers – or, presumably, hit on the head by pheasants falling out of the sky. The keepers at Holkham still wear these hats today.

The shoot is still largely of wild birds and most of the days are taken by the family, but it is also part of a general spirit of enterprise that pervades the estate: for Holkham, besides being a family home, is also a business and must pay for itself, through tourism, agriculture, film location, the nursery and its various shops.

Agricultural Innovators

The Cokes are best known historically for their contribution to agriculture. Thomas William Coke is credited with introducing a number of revolutionary new systems, but

Right: The richness of decoration in Holkham continues without abate from room to room.

more recent commentators have suggested that all he actually did was to make farming fashionable for the aristocracy, a class for whom labour of any kind had previously been anathema. It was his son, the second earl, who made a far more practical contribution to agriculture.

On Public Display

Many of the best rooms of Holkham are open to the public. The Marble Hall, with its 50-foot-high ceilings, marble statues and alabaster walls (there is actually very little marble in it, despite its name) is a spectacular introduction to this vast and imposing house. The alabaster for the hall was brought laboriously here by canal and sea, and the plaster ceilings are the work of the great London master plasterer Thomas Clark.

The North State Sitting Room has beautiful marble chimneypieces and 18th-century Brussels tapestries of the sun moving through the signs of the zodiac; but curiously, the set is incomplete. The Palladian Statue Gallery, long, elegant and beautifully lit, is filled with marble 18th-century copies of Greek and Roman statues. Gentlemen visitors in earlier times are said to

Left: *Marble statuary elegantly guiding you through passageways only serve to add to the feeling that you are somewhere really very special at Holkham Hall.*

have forbidden their wives to enter the gallery as the statues are naked.

The Green State Bedroom has rich Soho and Brussels tapestries of scenes from Europe, Asia, Africa and America, and a fine 18th-century painting of Jupiter Caressing Juno by William Hamilton. This bedroom was always offered to visiting monarchs; but if a queen or princess happened to be staying the Jupiter picture, considered rather risqué in earlier times, was moved for the duration; while for kings and other distinguished male visitors it was allowed to stay in the position

it occupies today, above the fireplace.

Though it was refitted in mid-Victorian times, the old kitchen dates largely from the 1750s. Today, with its massive cast-iron ovens and cabinets, it gives the visitor a chance to see how the kitchen in a big country house was organized and run; amazingly, this one continued in use until the Second World War, producing and serving more than 1,500 meals in an average month.

When you have seen the house it is time to enjoy the grounds with their splendid walks, shops and cafés.

Right: The double-height Marble Hall, much of which is actually alabaster, cannot fail to impress as one enters Holkham Hall

HOUGHTON HALL

Houghton Hall's greatest claim to fame is that it was built, early in the 18th century, for the man generally accepted as Britain's first Prime Minister, Sir Robert Walpole. The house – the embodiment of English Palladianism – has magnificent interiors by William Kent and is surrounded by parkland where a herd of fallow deer has been selectively bred over many years so that the animals are now pure white. In 1741, the park at Houghton was 6 miles round with a herd of 1,500 fallow deer. Deer numbers have dropped to about 1,000 head, but the herd remains unique in this parkland context. The estate borders the Queen's estate at Sandringham and the current owners of the house, the Cholmondeleys (who have lived here since 1797) have other royal connections: the marquesses of Cholmondeley traditionally hold the post of Lord Great Chamberlain, for example.

Opulence and Simplicity

Building at Houghton began in 1722 to designs by Colin Campbell, but the house was not completed until six years after his death in 1735, by which time the original design had been substantially altered by architects Thomas Ripley and James Gibbs.

Built in a beautiful grey stone brought especially from Yorkshire, the house is a curious mix of magnificent opulence in the

***Below:** A Palladian palace in Norfolk, built for Britain's first Prime Minister, Robert Walpole.*

state rooms and relative simplicity in the family's own apartments.

Perhaps the grandest of all the rooms at Houghton is the Saloon. With its high coved ceiling it retains its original Kent designs and is populated by gods and goddesses disporting themselves in sylvan scenes in the painted decoration, the plasterwork and the carving. Central to this opulent display is the octagonal painting in the centre of the ceiling showing Apollo driving his chariot of the sun.

Exquisite Interiors

The White Drawing Room has changed dramatically over the years, but there is still a beautiful lapis lazuli table designed by Kent as well as splendid 18th-century silk hangings. The Stone Hall is perhaps the most impressive room in the house, rising to double height with a gallery; the idea is based on Inigo Jones's designs for the Queen's House at Greenwich. The sculpture and carving are by J.M. Rysbrack, who came to England from the Low Countries in 1720. Six benches were designed specifically for the hall and, along with two tables, they remain to this day.

The Tapestry Dressing Room was originally known as the Van Dyck Dressing Room. It contains five beautiful 17th-century tapestries showing Charles I and Henrietta Maria, James I and his wife Anne of Denmark, and Christian IV of Denmark.

The Green Velvet Bedchamber contains one of Houghton's great treasures – a bed designed by William Kent whose hangings alone cost more than £1,200, a colossal sum at the time. The Brussels tapestries depicting 'The Loves of Venus and Adonis' were commissioned specifically for the panels in the four corners of the room.

The Embroidered Bedchamber contains the second state bed, which was made in about 1730 and is hung with oriental needlework. The set of green velvet and walnut chairs has always been in this room.

The beautiful Marble Parlour is one of the least changed parts of the house. One of its interesting features is the neat arrangement by which the entrance for servants was positioned behind the chimney breast. The ceiling paintings show Bacchus, the god of wine, and bunches of grapes appear throughout the room on the frieze, the beams and the fireplace, the doorcases, pierglass and tables. The chairs here date from 1715 and the 16-foot-long table is original to the room.

Below: *The Stone Hall is an awe-inspiring cube of grandeur, with an elaborate gallery and ceiling.*

A Glimpse Behind the Scenes

The Common Parlour gives the visitor a rare glimpse (the only glimpse, in fact) into the private rooms as opposed to the state rooms. The impression here is of simplicity rather than grandeur. Above the fireplace, in a beautifully carved wooden frame, is a portrait of Sir Robert Walpole's brother, Galfridus; also here are various Cholmondeley family portraits, including Pompeo Batoni's portrait of the first Marquess of Cholmondeley.

One of Houghton's more unusual attractions is the extraordinary Cholmondeley Soldier Museum, containing more than 22,000 model soldiers from famous historical battles.

Below: The Walpole Coat of Arms, at the centre of the Stone Hall's magnificent stucco ceiling by Giuseppe Artari.

BURGHLEY HOUSE

The history of great houses is also inevitably the history of the great titles which map the advancement of the landed families of England to whom they belonged. The Cecils of Burghley House, beginning as minor Lincolnshire gentry, rose to become knights, then barons, then earls and finally marquesses; and it was William Cecil, who was born in 1520, who first acquired the name by which his great country house in Lincolnshire is known.

From Cecil to Burghley

Cecil rose to become the most powerful man in the kingdom and Queen Elizabeth I's most trusted and longest-serving adviser. His survival amid the intrigue of the Elizabethan court for more than 40 years is nothing short of astonishing and a tribute to his diplomatic skills. But he was not just Elizabeth's most trusted minister; he was also one of her closest friends, and when he lay dying in 1598 she apparently sat by his bedside and insisted on personally feeding him the thin soup that was all he was able to eat.

For his loyal service William was created Lord Burghley in 1571, and with the title came great wealth – wealth sufficient to construct the massive house at Stamford that is his greatest monument. Built a generation before Audley End, Burghley House still looks to the arriving visitor much as it would have done when completed in 1587. Cecil oversaw the building and insisted on a wonderful mix of the classical – then just coming into fashion in England – and the Tudor.

Below: *Burghley is far more than a country house; it is an Elizabethan palace on a scale that surpassed the expectations of its founder, Queen Elizabeth I's favourite, Lord Burghley.*

The house took nearly 20 years to build, and when it was finished, though Cecil also had a house in London and an even more spectacular one in Hertfordshire – Theobalds, now long gone – he always considered Burghley House the family seat, despite the fact that he was to spend so little time there. Burghley is the biggest surviving house of the early Elizabethan period; it is also externally one of the least altered. Inside, of course, it is a different story, and the influence of changing fashion is evident throughout; nevertheless, the changes introduced by Cecil's descendants – who still live at the house – are not so extensive that the origins of the house have been completely obscured.

Opposite: This spectacularly intricate gate was built to reflect the importance of its original owner, William Cecil.

From Across the Continent

The greatest changes occurred after the title passed to John Cecil in 1678. At this time the fashion for all things continental was at its height and John, by now fifth Earl of Exeter, spent several years travelling across Europe buying huge numbers of pictures, sculptures and other works of art. At immense cost – a cost that almost bankrupted the family – he brought these to Burghley, where they remain to this day. The paintings at Burghley, a collection to which he made the biggest contribution, are said to represent the greatest single collection of Italian art outside Italy. Not content with the amounts he had already spent, John was determined that the house should be modernized in order to provide the right setting for his acquisitions.

The most spectacular rooms in the house include the Pagoda Room, with its royal portraits (Henry VIII and Elizabeth I, as well as a beautiful picture presumed to be Mary, Queen of Scots); the Queen Elizabeth Room (though she never stayed in the house); and the Marquetry Room, which contains a superb picture by Peter Brueghel the Younger showing village rent day. The Billiard Room has a magnificent portrait of the 10th earl by Sir Thomas Lawrence.

Heaven and Hell

Perhaps the most remarkable rooms in a generally remarkable house are the Heaven Room and Hell Staircase. The walls and ceilings of both were painted by the 17th-century Italian artist Antonio Verrio, who lived at the house for many years and ran up huge debts in the local inns and alehouses. What makes Verrio's painting in the Heaven Room, showing gods and goddesses disporting themselves, particularly outstanding is that it is painted in the trompe l'œil style, creating an illusion of three dimensions that is entirely convincing. Beyond the Heaven Room, the dark, forbidding Hell Staircase shows the fiery pit as a huge cat's mouth, and Death with his scythe. All around the tormented suffer eternal agonies.

Among the highlights beyond the house are Capability Brown's beautiful 26-acre lake (dug to look like a meandering river), the Orangery and the splendid Lion Bridge.

Family History

By the early 19th century the family's great days at court were long over (though the earls of Salisbury remained politically active into the 20th century), but the Cecils were still among the country's leading families and owned substantial lands: Burghley House still stands amid some 10,000 acres. So when Henry, the 10th earl and now Marquess of Exeter, married a Shropshire farmer's daughter in 1801 he provoked the general outrage of the aristocracy. The chief claim to fame of Henry's son Brownlow was that he spent a fortune making Burghley even grander than it already was in preparation for a visit by Queen Victoria and Prince Albert. The ruinously expensive bed he bought for them can still be seen in what is now known as the Second George Room.

The sixth marquess, David, earned his place in history by winning a gold medal at the 1928 Olympics in the men's 400m Hurdles.

DEENE PARK

The Brudenells have lived at Deene Park since 1514. Traces of the original medieval manor remain, but what we see today is largely 16th-century with Georgian additions. The medieval manor was owned by Westminster Abbey before the de Deens acquired the house in the 13th century, followed by the Tyndales in the 15th century and then the Littons, who sold the manor to Robert Brudenell, direct ancestor of the current owners. Few estates have had so few owners over such a long period; but, like most old families, the Brudenells have altered and adapted the house down the centuries.

Right: *Deene Park's most famous owner and the subject of this portrait, Lord Cardigan, was the hero of the Charge of the Light Brigade in 1854.*

Previous page: *Deene Park is surrounded by beautiful grounds and an attractive lake, beside which visitors are welcome to picnic.*

A House of Eccentrics

Deene Park is built round a courtyard, but the exterior has something of a Gothic appearance today, with castellations and towers typical of that vaguely fortified medieval look beloved of the early 19th century. Its most famous owner was undoubtedly James, seventh Earl of Cardigan, who in 1854 took part in one of the great military disasters of the Crimean War – the Charge of the Light Brigade. The house still contains the uniforms, medals and other memorabilia he brought back from the war – including, bizarrely, the stuffed and mounted head of Ronald, the horse he rode at the Charge.

The earl's wife, the famously eccentric Lady Adeline, outlived her husband by almost half a century (she died in 1915). She kept her own coffin in the house so she could check regularly that it would fit, and when her husband died she immediately commissioned her own death mask. Perhaps her most endearing habit was cycling into the village wearing her late husband's regimental trousers.

Apart from war memorabilia, Deene Park's lofty, spacious rooms are filled with family and other portraits and good early furniture.

Right: *Much of Deene Park retains the feel of a Tudor mansion.*

Left: *The formal gardens at Deene Park.*

Below: *Deene Park is a comfortable house despite its grand history.*

CANONS ASHBY

Canons Ashby takes its name from the Augustinian priory that existed in this little-visited but very beautiful part of Northamptonshire. The house is better known, however, for its associations with the great 17th-century poet laureate John Dryden, whose descendants' relatives lived at Canons Ashby until it was given to the National Trust in 1981.

Below: *Canons Ashby's quirky and charming south elevation.*

The Dryden Residence

The house is by no means grand, but this is part of its charm. It was always a house of the minor gentry, the squirearchy. The first Dryden recorded as living here arrived in 1551, having inherited what was then a

farmhouse through his wife. He added to the property substantially, making the L-shaped building into an H-shaped house. John's son Erasmus built onto the H-shape to create a closed courtyard – the present Pebble Court.

Through succeeding generations other Drydens added beautiful plaster ceilings or commissioned murals for the walls or splendid fireplaces, but none undertook any substantial demolition or structural replacement work. The past was always left in place to complement new work, which is why the house today presents such a fascinating mix of styles.

The oldest part of the house is the east range, where massive oak cruck beams (the earliest form of timber framing) support what is almost certainly the original late medieval farmhouse. Now given over to more functional concerns – the pump room and brewery – this eastern part of the house leads through to the Pebble Court (which gets its name from the sea-smooth stones fixed into the ground).

A Haphazard Development

Once inside the house the visitor is struck by the wonderful asymmetry of everything – bricked-up windows, corridors in odd places and crooked corners all bear witness to the delightfully haphazard way in which the house developed.

Below: The dining room's panelling and simple fireplace reflect the modest status of the local squirearchy.

Opposite: *The Drawing Room's ornate plasterwork domed ceiling was added in the 1630s; its richness matched only by the glorious fireplace, which dates back to the 1590s.*

Below: *The Book Room was added to Canons Ashby by Erasmus Dryden in about 1590, but its present appearance can be attributed to Sir Henry Dryden, who designed the oak bookcases.*

The Public and the Private

Among the most remarkable rooms is the Winter Parlour, which probably looks now exactly as it did in the 1580s. The beautiful walnut panelling, which has survived restoration and remodelling (and also woodworm, to which walnut was always especially prone), is covered with proverbs, sayings and heraldic decoration – the emblems and shields of the Drydens and all the local families with which they had connections.

The Winter Parlour would have been one of the family's private rooms. More public – in fact, the showpiece room of the house – was the Hall, with its tall mullioned windows, where guests would have dined with the family. More recently, the room was used as a billiard room, but the two blocked-up doors to the kitchen and buttery can still be seen. The room has a good 17th-century scaglioli table (a kind of imitation marble), a large painting of cannons and muskets above the mantelpiece and a set of very early leather fire-buckets.

The kitchen, substantially unaltered since the late 16th century, still has the servants' bells high up on the walls, and a Victorian range has been fitted. The worn flagstones are eloquent of countless generations of servants' feet.

The Dining Room has a more modern

In 1985, the Russell
Père David's deer
deer originated, the
that a communis
reintroducing it. The
the deer – a Russell

Great Collectors

The Russells have always b
collectors, which explains why th
filled with exquisite furniture and
the early 18th century, while on
Tour of Europe, the fourth Duke
commissioned a number of picture
great Venetian painter Canaletto,
now hang in the splendid Venetia

Despite its name, Woburn Ab
no trace of its earlier existence as
foundation, although we know
present courtyard stands on what
the abbey cloisters.

Russell family members are reco

Above: *This elegant early 18th-century tall-backed walnut chair sits between trompe l'oeil columns in the Painted Parlour, which was created by Elizabeth Creed (1642–1728).*

Right: *This opulent bedroom was once used by Queen Victoria in 1841, hence it is filled with paintings by her favourite artists.*

the 1950s the rest of the house remains substantially unaltered since the 1750s.

On Public View

The 20 rooms open to visitors include the State Dining Room, with its numerous portraits; the gold and silver vaults, where work by great silversmiths, including Paul de Lamerie, is on display (the silver teapots are still used by the family); and Queen Victoria's bedroom, where there are pictures by Sir Edwin Landseer and Sir George Hayter, two of her most favoured artists. Here, too, there are etchings, copies of drawings made by Queen Victoria during her stay in 1841 and presented to the then Duchess of Bedford.

The park surrounding the house still extends to more than 3,000 acres and is said to be the least altered example of the work of Humphry Repton, who was commissioned to landscape the grounds in 1802 and added a lake, a bridge and a meandering river. There are ten species of deer in the park including, of course, those beautiful Père David deer. The famous Woburn Safari Park helps bring in much-needed income for the continual programme of restoration.

Left: *The simplicity of Woburn Abbey's exterior is just an element of the gracefulness of the entire house.*

Below: *The rooms at Woburn, although filled with rare and expensive pieces of China and paintings, manage to retain a feeling of domesticity.*

CLAYDON HOUSE

Claydon House is by no means among the best known of the National Trust's properties. It was never a great palace like Blenheim or Hatfield; but its interior is uniquely beautiful and extraordinary, and it has been home to the Verney family for more than three and a half centuries.

Dismissal and Disagreement

Building by the second Lord Verney began in 1757, but the carcass of a much earlier house – probably Jacobean – exists beneath the present façade. A huge west wing was begun by Luke Lightfoot but problems with money led to his dismissal. Thomas Robinson took over, but then he quarrelled with Earl Verney in 1771 and left, after which the work continued under William Donn. However, Lightfoot was employed for long enough to complete the Oriental and rococo work on view today. What remains is just one section of the original house, but it is filled with rooms decorated in what was then the first flowering of a passion for all things eastern.

The main motifs of the white woodwork decorative scheme are pagodas, oriental birds and exquisite summer-houses. The decoration includes some of the best woodcarving in

Europe, and it reaches its climax in the Chinese Room – without question the most extraordinary room in the house. Lightfoot's intricate figures will stand comparison with almost anything by Grinling Gibbons.

The parquetry staircase – inlaid with what would have been extremely expensive ebony and ivory – is justly famous. The wrought iron balustrade is decorated with ears of corn so delicate they are said to rustle as visitors pass by!

Haunted House

Claydon is also said to be haunted by the ghost of Sir Edmund Verney, who apparently wanders around looking for his hand, buried here after he died in 1642 at the Battle of Edgehill, in which he was standard bearer to the king. The rest of his body was never found.

Florence Nightingale – a relative of the Verney family – was a frequent visitor to Claydon, and mementoes of her life and work in the Crimea can be seen in the room in which she slept.

Outside, the park sweeps down to three beautiful lakes, the home of giant bronze-coloured carp and dangerous pike. There is a small church and a delightful garden walk.

Above: The Chinese Room has some of the most extraordinary woodcarving to be found anywhere in Europe. Carried out by one man, Luke Lightfoot, the decoration is rococo at its most extravagant.

BLENHEIM PALACE

Military leadership seems to run in the Churchill family to an extraordinary degree. The family home – if a house as big as Blenheim can be described as a home – is named after the site of one of the most important 18th-century military victories. The said battle took place in 1704 on the Danube near the village of Blindheim. At the end of the battle, John Churchill, first Duke of Marlborough, had defeated the forces of Louis XIV and French attempts to dominate Europe were at an end.

Below: There is little doubt as to why Blenheim describes itself as a palace rather than as a mere house, and it was always intended as such – a statement rather than a sanctuary.

A Battle Remembered

A grateful nation, in the person of Queen Anne, gave the duke the royal manor of Woodstock, just a few miles from Oxford. She also agreed to build him a house, to be known as Blenheim in memory of the great battle, at her own expense. Building began in 1705 but was not completed until 1722: intrigues at court caused the supply of money to dry up, and eventually Churchill had to use his own funds to finish the work.

The designer was the architect and playwright Sir John Vanbrugh, whose style is usually described as that of the English baroque – generally distinguished from continental baroque in that where the latter relied on ornate and elaborate decoration, the English form depended on sheer size to achieve the same imposing effects. This is certainly true at Blenheim.

A Formidable Building

There is nothing cozy or domestic about this large, low-built house, said to be the biggest

domestic building in Britain. It sits above a lake spanned by a triumphal bridge which is almost as imposing as the house itself. Perhaps the grandest room in a house in which all the rooms are magnificent is the 180-foot Long Library, with its extraordinary stucco ceiling decoration. The Long Library, designed originally as a picture gallery, was unquestionably built to impress.

Three apartments interconnect between the Long Library and the Saloon. These are known as the First, Second and Third State Rooms. The First State Room, filled with superb tapestries and pictures, also displays a despatch written to Queen Anne from the battlefield at Blenheim pronouncing victory.

Arguably the most interesting picture in the house is the huge portrait of the fourth Duke of Marlborough and his family, painted in 1778 by Sir Joshua Reynolds and hung in the Red Drawing Room.

Blenheim must always have been difficult to live in – Voltaire once said that if the rooms had been as wide as the walls were thick it would have been convenient enough. Vanbrugh's idea was to have the living rooms in a central block with kitchens in one side block and stables in the other, but spreading the functions of the house in this way meant a long journey from kitchen to dining room.

Left: The interiors match the palatial architecture of the exterior; many of the tapestries illustrate the Duke of Marlborough's military successes.

BROUGHTON CASTLE

*Apart from selecting rising ground, early house-builders often looked for a position with
a ready supply of water – which almost certainly explains the position of the original
Broughton Castle, built by Sir John de Broughton at the close of the Middle Ages. He chose a
spot where three streams meet, which must have made construction of the 3-acre moat –
considered essential in the still unsettled England of the late 13th century – relatively easy.*

A Castle by Crenellation

We know that the original castle was under construction, if not complete, by 1300, and much of the present house – and the moat – dates back to that time. There was probably an earlier house on the site, but nothing of it survives. By 1377, the castle had passed into the hands of William of Wykeham, the then Bishop of Winchester. William of Wykeham's great-nephew Thomas inherited the house, which eventually went to his granddaughter, Margaret. Margaret married

William Fiennes, the second Lord Saye and Sele. Wykeham's descendants still live at Broughton today – a remarkable record of occupation by one family.

The work of transforming the medieval house he had inherited began in 1406, when Sir Thomas applied for and was granted permission to crenellate his house – a privilege afforded only to those of high rank and granted only by the reigning monarch. Sir Richard Fiennes, William's grandson, began to build the two floors above the Great Hall, and

to rebuild the west wing above the medieval kitchens; this work was completed by Sir Richard's son, also Richard, between 1550 and 1600. An anonymous but clearly exceptional master plasterer was commissioned to create the elaborate and beautifully preserved plaster ceiling which still exists in the Great Parlour.

By the early 17th century, the family had become prominent in political circles, the Puritan sympathizer William Fiennes siding with the parliamentarians against Charles I. Broughton became a centre of political intrigue, and for a time the anti-royalist faction met here; but after the King was executed, a disapproving Fiennes abandoned his political career and retired to Lundy Island in the Bristol Channel, which he also owned.

The House Abandoned

The huge changes in fashion that took place in England at the end of the 17th century and throughout the 18th seem to have left Broughton relatively untouched, perhaps because the Fiennes family preferred to live at their house at Belvedere in Kent, which was of course closer to London and the centre of fashion.

By the time Queen Victoria came to the throne in 1837, Broughton was in a poor state: its rooms empty, the roof beginning to leak, the walls festooned with thick ivy. All the furniture had been sold in a vast auction that lasted more than a week. To one traveller the place had a ghostly, forbidding aspect and looked as if it were rapidly returning to nature.

There was no money in the family to spend on repairing Broughton, for William Thomas Fiennes, the son of the 14th Lord Saye and Sele, had spent the lot gambling and carousing with his friend the Prince Regent – and yet, ironically, it may well be that we have this spendthrift to thank for the preservation of the house. There is no doubt that repair at this point would have meant transformation or demolition and rebuilding, the fate of so many medieval houses whose owners had enough money to keep up with changes in fashion. As it turned out, it was not until the 1860s that repairs were carried out, with the help of the Victorian architect George Gilbert Scott junior, and by the late 20th century the house's future was secure, supported by substantial grants from English Heritage and other bodies.

Of course, despite superficial appearances, the house has changed over the years: there was the disastrous sale of its contents in the early 19th century, and repairs, additions and restorations – relatively minor – are visible from all eras.

Educated and Erudite

Any tour should start in the room that has always been at the centre of the house: the Great Hall. The core of this room is the original medieval hall, but with the additions of 16th-century windows and a mid-18th-century plaster ceiling. At the west end of the hall a door would have led to the medieval kitchens. Above the splendid fireplace is a portrait of William of Wykeham, founder of New College, Oxford, from whose sister the family is descended; and there are excellent pictures of William, first Viscount Saye, who led the opposition to Charles I, and Nathaniel, William's second son, who became Speaker of the House of Lords. Equally fascinating are the 18th-century leather water-buckets – essential in those pre-fire-brigade days.

The Dining Room, originally the undercroft, takes us back to the very earliest days of the house, for here we see the original late 14th-century stone vaulted ceilings. The room now has a 15th-century fireplace, very beautiful double-linenfold panelling and Regency chairs. It is worth keeping an eye out for the carved heads beneath the ceiling arches in the passageway that leads out beyond the dining room.

The Oak Room, on the ground floor of the west wing, has a beautifully carved porchway on which is inscribed in Latin *Quod olim fuit meminisse minime iuvat* ('There is no pleasure in remembering the past'). The porchway probably dates to the 1660s. There is also a fine portrait which may be of Mrs Nathaniel Fiennes, the mother of Celia Fiennes. Celia was one of the most remarkable members of the Fiennes family: at the end of the 17th century, she set off across Britain on horseback and then wrote a book about her travels – a most unusual thing for a woman to do at the time. For historians, Celia's book is still an important source of information about 17th-century England.

Royal Rooms

The King's Chamber has one of the best fireplaces in the house – elaborate and magnificently carved with dryads, it

Below: With its moat, Broughton Castle echoes an earlier period when political conflict ensured that defence features really were essential.

Right: The Great Hall
initially appears to be a mass
of cold stone and unwelcoming
armour, but look up and you
will discover a fine plasterwork
ceiling.

probably dates to the mid-16th century and illustrates a tale from Ovid's *Metamorphoses*. The Great Parlour has its unsurpassed plaster ceiling carved with the date 1599 and the initials of Richard and Elizabeth Fiennes incorporated in the design. The Council Chamber, a small room at the top of the west stairs, was named thus as it was where the opponents of Charles I used to meet.

Anne of Denmark, who married King James I, is said to have slept at Broughton in 1604; the room she occupied now bears her name, and a portrait of her hangs above the fireplace. A stone staircase leads to the exquisite 14th-century chapel, still with its original encaustic floor tiles and its altar.

Outside the house the grounds have much to recommend them, not least the beautiful gatehouse which was probably completed in about 1400. The Walled Garden – known as the Ladies' Garden – dates back to the 1880s and is filled with roses. The 14th-century parish church of St Mary, a short distance away, is filled with Fiennes and Wykeham memorials.

CHASTLETON HOUSE

Chastleton has many claims to fame, yet for a long time it was a forgotten house, unregarded by historians of architecture and little visited. It is a relatively small yet perfect Jacobean house, never restored or added to, never really modernized and entirely untouched – and this includes its park – by the 18th-century enthusiasts. This, of course, is why it was for so long deeply unfashionable; the sort of house that could easily have been swept away at any time in the past. The fact that such a house survived unscathed is a tribute to the instincts – and the comparative poverty – of the family that lived here for so long.

Shabby Charm

Chastleton was always a family home and, perhaps as a direct result of this, it has retained something that few far grander houses possess: a mass of early everyday objects as well as the sort of grand pieces you would expect in a more palatial house. Chastleton (which, incidentally, is where the rules of English croquet were first agreed in 1865) was also one of the first houses that the National Trust decided not to restore to pristine condition. What that means is that Chastleton has a lived-in air; almost an air of ancient shabbiness, but it is all the more enchanting for that.

The house, which was completed in 1612

Below: The warm Cotswold sandstone and simple symmetry of Chastleton only ever seems to improve with age, and Chastleton is almost four centuries old.

Below: The Long Gallery's barrel-vaulted Jacobean plasterwork ceiling was constructed from a conventional armature of ribs and split laths. No other contemporary ceiling like this has survived.

on land once owned by the Gunpowder Plot conspirator Robert Catesby, was built originally for Walter Jones, a wealthy lawyer. The Jones family stayed for more than four centuries before the house passed, with funds supplied by a number of charities, to the National Trust in 1991. Its decision to focus on preservation rather than restoration means the contents and fabric of the building are very fragile; hence visitors have to be kept to limited numbers and pre-booking is essential.

Golden Grandeur

The Cotswold stone house has a fortified look about it: three stories are enlivened by numerous gables, and the staircase is contained in a castellated tower. Among the few improvements made by the family was the installation of a flushing lavatory in 1830 – considered daring and unhygienic at the time. Even the gigantic ladder built specially to reach the roof and gutters is still here! Little has been added and little taken away.

Yet, despite the relatively humble nature of the house – the family were minor gentry – there are spectacular features: the Long Gallery at the top of the house (mostly used by the family for running up and down in winter for exercise when the weather was bad) has a curved plaster ceiling of spectacular beauty.

Surprising Survivors

A screened passage leads into the Hall, the best room in the house, hung with 17th-century family portraits. Creaking corridors lead into other rooms and passageways past oak and early furniture. Many of the beautiful tapestries and other wall hangings are still where they were placed when the house was built; among the most interesting is a panel of Dornix, a kind of striped damask, found on the upper floor landing. Even today it shines brightly and has hardly faded, its stripes of white, red, yellow and

Below: *Chastleton has an Elizabethan–Jacobean garden with a fabulous ring of topiary that encompasses all sorts of figures, from a cat to a galleon.*

blue almost as bright now as when it was new.

Extraordinary Flanders tapestries – again original to the house – can be found in the Fettiplace Room, and examples of rare flame-stitch embroidery in a small anteroom.

Lost in the War

The family's own sense of history can be judged by the often-repeated tale of the last Jones, who lived at Chastleton in the 1940s. Mrs Irene Whitmore-Jones used to tell visitors that the Joneses lost their money in the war; given that this was in the late 1940s, the unwary thought she meant the war just ended. In fact, she was referring to the English Civil Wars three centuries earlier! Arthur Jones had sided with the King and was fined by Cromwell for so doing. At one time he was even pursued to the house by parliamentary forces. He hid in a small room above the entrance porch while – so it is said

– his wife offered the soldiers plenty of food and drink laced with a sleep-inducing drug. When they were out cold her husband made good his escape.

Among the fascinating and contrasting details of this house are the copy of the bible Charles I had with him on the scaffold at Whitehall and a 1940s Pye radio; at the end of a beautiful early tester bed there is an old electric hot-water bottle, and cupboards are still filled with preserves and bottles of sloe gin. Other store rooms contain old bottles, election posters, a slipper bath and a bizarre indoor exercise machine that was meant to mimic the action of riding a horse.

The house overlooks a quiet valley – and even that has an ancient, unmodernized feel to it – and the gardens include a beautiful Astronomical Garden, a lake with an island, a Gertrude Jekyll-inspired herbaceous border and – of course – a croquet lawn.

Right: The hall at Chastleton House has an impressive art installation in the form of a two-dimensional deer with real antlers attached.

COUGHTON COURT

Ancient English Catholic families who retained their ancestral homes despite centuries of persecution are very rare in England. One thinks of the Stonors at Stonor Park, where mass has been celebrated continuously since the 13th century; and of the remarkable Throckmortons, whose estate at Coughton – including the great house, two churches and many outbuildings – survives relatively complete in the countryside just to the south of Birmingham.

Previous page: *Coughton Court was originally a Tudor courtyard house, which underwent alterations after suffering damage during the English Civil War.*

Below: *The Gothic west elevation encloses a grand central gatehouse. It is a wonderful mix of architectural styles.*

Catholics at Coughton

The Throckmortons have been here since 1409, and the present house – completed in the 1530s under the watchful eye of Sir George Throckmorton – may have replaced an earlier medieval building. Originally a courtyard house, Coughton now has three sides only, the fourth or east range having been destroyed by an anti-Catholic mob in the late 17th century.

The eastern side had included the family's private chapel and was therefore particularly vulnerable at a time when Catholics were viewed at the very least with suspicion and more often with open hostility. The east wing was never rebuilt, and its absence means that today the old courtyard opens on to gardens that run down to the River Arrow. The original moat was filled in in the late 18th century.

The entrance front, with its centrally placed tower gatehouse (the oldest part of the house) is beautifully constructed from a local honey-coloured stone. It conceals a wealth of Elizabethan half-timbered brick structures which are visible only from the back of the house, for Coughton is one of those grand houses whose charm lies largely in the

accretion without destruction of the work of many periods and many styles.

The Gunpowder Plot

The most famous – or infamous – Throckmorton was Robert Catesby, who took part in the disastrous Gunpowder Plot with Guy Fawkes. Catesby, who was killed while on the run for his part in the plot, was Thomas Throckmorton's nephew. A permanent exhibition about the plot and the family's role in it is housed in one of Coughton's stables.

Sir George Throckmorton, who died in 1553, opposed Henry VIII's decision to divorce Catherine of Aragon and make himself head of the church. For the Throckmortons, the Dissolution of the Monasteries and the break with Rome marked the beginning of three centuries of internal exile. More immediately, Sir George was forced to provide a home for his aunt, Elizabeth, the former abbess of the convent at Denny. Elizabeth brought with her a carved dole-gate, through which help had traditionally been given to the poor from inside the convent. The gate is carved with Elizabeth's name and is a rare pre-

Reformation survival. It now takes pride of place in the dining room.

Traitors Hidden

For generations the Throckmortons were to be persecuted for their Catholicism. They were regularly fined and Coughton Court was frequently searched, particularly during the Elizabethan period, for evidence of treason. A priest hole still exists in the house and there is no doubt that the family never really reconciled themselves to the Protestant succession. Francis Throckmorton, a nephew, was executed in 1584 for carrying messages between Mary, Queen of Scots and the Spanish ambassador, 20 years before the Gunpowder Plot.

Even when they weren't getting into trouble for their faith, the Throckmortons seemed to court difficulties of one sort or another – the daughter of Sir Nicholas Throckmorton, for example, secretly married Sir Walter Ralegh, one of Elizabeth I's favourites, and was banished from court. Sir Nicholas's portrait hangs in the house.

Coughton contains numerous reminders of the family's Catholic faith, including a book called *Tabula Eliensis* in the Tower Room. This bears the Throckmorton coat of arms and the coats of arms of all the Catholic gentry imprisoned for recusancy during Elizabeth I's reign. It is dated 1596.

Fluctuating Fortunes

The Throckmortons' fortunes revived a little under Charles I as the Stuarts were staunch believers in an absolutist monarchy: Robert Throckmorton was made a baronet by Charles I in 1642. After the victory of the parliamentarians, Coughton was taken from the family – sequestrated, to use the technical jargon – but it was restored to them when Charles II returned from exile. Repairs following damage inflicted on the house during the Civil War were under way when, in 1688, a Protestant mob from Alcester burned down the Catholic chapel and the whole of the east wing.

The recusancy laws were abolished in 1792, and the Catholic Emancipation Act of 1829 meant that Sir Robert George Throckmorton, eighth baronet, could become an MP: the first Throckmorton actively engaged in public life for almost three centuries.

By the mid-20th century the general costs of upkeep were bearing heavily on Coughton, as on so many English country houses. As a result the family gave the house to the National Trust in 1946, on condition that they should continue to live in the house for 300 years and retain the chattels. In 1990–95 the family, entirely at their own expense, restored the house in its entirety and began to open it more frequently.

Architecture and Antiques

The house today has much to interest visitors, in terms of both contents and architecture. The gatehouse tower with its octagonal battlemented turrets and two-storey oriel window leads into the hall, which soars to ornate fan vaulting. Above the tower's entrance archway can also be seen the arms of the Throckmortons and those of Henry VIII. The Gothic wings either side of the gatehouse were added in the late 18th century when the moat was filled in. The battlements were added in the 1830s and some years later a new Catholic chapel was built nearby.

Among the most interesting items in the house are family documents relating to the lives of an aristocratic recusant family and the magnificent 17th-century veneered mass cabinet with its secret cupboard for the Host. The chemise worn by Mary, Queen of Scots at her execution is also here (in the small room adjacent to the Dining Room), together with locks of hair cut from the Old and Young Pretenders; a cope embroidered, allegedly, by Catherine of Aragon; and a chair said to be made from the bed in which Richard III spent his last night before the Battle of Bosworth. There is also the bizarre Newbury Coat, which exists as a result of a bet made in 1811 between Sir John Throckmorton and a friend that a woollen coat could not be made (from sheep to garment) in one day. Sir John won the bet after a Mr Coxeter of Newbury in Berkshire had the sheep shorn at 5am and the wool woven and cut into cloth and made up into a coat by dinnertime that same day. There are

Opposite: Among the 25 acres that surround Coughton Court there is a knot garden, a wonderful rose labyrinth (seen here) and even a bog garden.

splendid family portraits from Tudor times and a superbly carved 15th-century alabaster tablet showing the Nativity – another remarkable survival of the Reformation destruction. Exceptionally good panelling can be seen in the dining room, and there is a magnificent chimneypiece in marble and timber.

Coughton Court has 25 acres of gardens with a lake. As part of their restorations in the 1990s, the family have given Coughton a completely new garden including an Elizabethan knot garden, an old walled garden with a rose labyrinth, a bog garden, an orchard (growing mostly traditional local varieties of apple and pear) and a delightful walk along the River Arrow. Christina Williams, daughter of Clare Throckmorton, is responsible for all the designs.

EASTNOR CASTLE

Eastnor Castle is a good example of a Georgian house pretending to be a medieval fortress. Perched above its lake amid the beauty of the Malvern Hills it has a rugged, impregnable exterior combined with delicate Italianate (and some Gothic) interiors. It was built by Robert Smirke (1752–1845) in a sort of toned-down Gothic style described occasionally as Norman Revival.

Wealthy Wives

Construction of the castle was begun in 1810, but the Eastnor estate had been owned by the Cocks family since the 16th century. They added land and wealth to their holdings by marrying well – into the Somers family and later, at about the time the castle was built, into the wealthy Nash family of Worcestershire. It was this combined wealth that gave the first Earl Somers (recently raised from the barony he inherited from his father) the money to begin building the castle.

By any standards it was a huge undertaking. Nearly 20,000 tonnes of stone and mortar – the stone brought here by canal barge and mule – were used by

Below: The imposing front elevation of Eastnor Castle. The mass of stonework and its simple design create a visually dominant building.

hundreds of workmen who, legend has it, were kept working in shifts day and night for more than six years. A revolutionary approach was taken to some aspects of the building: the sandstone facing looks traditional enough, for example, but all the major beams used inside are cast iron rather than wood.

Smirke helped design the interiors and even the furniture, but only traces of his work survive – in the Dining Room, Red Hall and Staircase Hall. Of his furniture only the benches and chairs in the Entrance Hall and Great Hall remain.

In 1850 the architect renowned for his designs for the House of Lords, Augustus Welby Pugin, was called in by Earl Somers to create what is still regarded as the house's masterpiece. Known as the Gothic Drawing Room, it is Pugin's finest surviving domestic interior and designed in his high Gothic Revival style. There is a fascinating family tree above the fireplace, and the chandelier was considered such a fine piece it was displayed at the Great Exhibition in 1851.

Post-War Restoration

The last Lord Somers went to Australia in the 1920s, and Eastnor Castle was left unoccupied for several years. Plans to use it as a support facility during the Second World War were abandoned after the Blitz ended, and it was only when Elizabeth Somers Cocks and Benjamin Hervey-Bathurst (parents of the present owner) moved back into the Castle after the war that a process of restoration began.

The costs, at a time when country-house owners could expect little return on their investment, were huge, and the work took many years. As a result of the efforts of their son, James, and especially his former wife, Sarah, supported by grants from English Heritage, visitors can now see a range of wonderfully revived interiors, from the vast baronial Great Hall (60 feet high and originally created to look like a medieval banqueting hall) to the Red Hall, with its collection of medieval armour (amassed by the third earl), the State Dining Room (rather spoiled in the 1930s when Smirke's Gothic arches were removed) and, best of all, of course, the Gothic Drawing Room, which is much as it would have been in the 1850s shortly after being remodelled by Pugin.

Like most great houses, Eastnor now has to pay its way: so you can organize a conference here, get married in the Gothic Drawing Room or camp in the deer park.

Opposite: The High Gothic Drawing Room at Eastnor Castle is Pugin's finest surviving domestic interior.

Right: The restoration of the interiors began after the Second World War, and although this house is impressively grand, it still functions as a lived-in house.

STANWAY HOUSE

James, Lord Niedpath, comes from a family that would be considered remarkable by any standards, for the Neidpaths, also earls of Wemyss (pronounced 'Weems'), and their forebears have lived in the same mellow Tudor sandstone house in Gloucestershire since the 1530s. Indeed, the estate of Stanway, tucked away in a particularly leafy corner of the county, has changed hands only once in 1,260 years, which takes us back to the early eighth century. Little has been changed in 300 years and the various rooms, their walls hung with a full complement of family portraits, have an almost lived-in look.

An Anonymous Architect

Stanway was built by unknown hands on the typical 16th-century E-plan; its staircases, each tread made from a great solid triangle of native oak, seem somehow to meander rather than take you anywhere directly, and if you don't know your way it is quite easy to find yourself lost or to discover that, having imagined you were at one end of the house, you have actually ended up at the other. But for Lord Niedpath, who has written a short and highly entertaining history of Stanway, the house is as familiar as his own face: 'We don't know who built it,' he says, with a dramatic sweep of his arm, 'but we know a lot about how it came to be owned by the family.' Extremely knowledgeable about his family history, he works tirelessly on the upkeep and restoration of the house and grounds.

In 715, Stanway was given by two local Mercian magnates, Odo and Dodo, to the abbey of Tewkesbury. Four monks were established here, holding the land in what was known as frankalmoign – that is, in return for their prayers for the souls of the founders of the abbey and their descendants. In 1530, Sir William Tracy of nearby Toddington declared in his will that he relied for his salvation on faith, not on the prayers of the monks: in response his body was dug up and burned by

__Below:__ Unusually for such a grand house, the architect of Stanway House remains anonymous, but it is undoubtedly one of the Cotswold's greatest treasures.

the Church, an act which caused widespread and understandable revulsion.

William's younger son, Richard, used his influence to obtain from the abbot at Tewkesbury a lease on Stanway in 1533. On the expiry of Richard's male line in 1677, Stanway passed to the Toddington branch of the Tracys, and the last of these Tracys, Susan, married Francis Charteris, Lord Elcho, son of the seventh Earl of Wemyss, in 1771. The house has remained in the ownership of the earls of Wemyss since then.

Ancient Traditions

Visitors to the house are always fascinated by

the collection of 18th-century hair: apparently it was the custom for visitors to Stanway to leave a piece of their hair behind in an envelope as a memento of their stay. But if that is one ancient practice that has died out, there are several others at Stanway that are carried on to this day, one in particular being the business of collecting the tenants' rents in what is known as the Audit Room, using a special revolving table with a drawer for each tenant's rent book; this table was made in 1778.

The rent-collecting ceremony – almost universal on country estates before 1914 – is one of the last of its kind in the country,

Right: The magnificent chairs, Chippendale day beds and tables on display in Stanway House are still used by the Niedpath family, hence the lived-in feel of this splendid house.

requiring as it does the tenants of the various cottages and farms actually to come to the house and hand over their money in person. Each payment is placed in a special well in the centre of the table, which is fitted with secret compartments for notes and a secret catch to prevent unauthorized removals of money.

Ancient Artefacts

If the rent table is an extraordinary survival, so too is the shuffleboard in the great hall. One of the oldest in the world (probably made in 1620), it is 22 feet 10 inches long and made from one solid piece of oak; it even has its original brass counters. The game is played much as shove ha'penny on a larger scale.

In one of the rooms there is a very rare Chippendale exercise chair – a chair fitted with long thick springs: apparently Lord Niedpath's ancestors took their exercise by bouncing vigorously up and down on it. Elsewhere in the house are family portraits and a family tree of the household dogs.

Stanway is a Grade I Listed property, and the work of restoration and repair is almost continual – outside as well as in. The formal canal and cascade shown in a painting in the Great Hall have been partly restored since the mid-1990s and a 300-foot fountain, the second tallest in Europe, has been added.

Below: The rather forbidding Great Hall still has its 22-foot-and-10-inch-long shuffleboard.

OWLPEN MANOR

It is difficult to understand how our 18th- and 19th-century forebears could happily demolish dozens of late medieval and Tudor houses on the grounds that they were quaint and old-fashioned – precisely those qualities that we now value so highly. Fortunately, some survived these depredations; one of them is Owlpen, which deserves to be better known for it is the quintessence of Englishness.

A Cotswold Secret

This Tudor manor house – which began life in 1450 and has been little altered since about 1610 – sits in a quiet wooded valley in a remote area of the Cotswolds. Its name has nothing to do with owls – in Old English it means 'the land enclosed by Olla', presumably a chieftain. By the 12th century, the De Olepenne family were living here. Then in the early 15th century the house and land passed by marriage to the Daunt family, and was handed down generation after generation until 1805, when it passed by marriage into the Stoughton family. The last member of this long lineage died in 1924 (though various cadet branches of the Daunts have survived in Ireland and elsewhere).

In 1925 the estate was broken up and sold. By sheer good luck the old manor house, which by then had been empty for almost a century, was bought and carefully repaired by the Arts and Crafts architect Norman Jewson. Today Owlpen sits at the centre of a group of historic buildings, including a mill of 1728 and a group of cottages, some of which are available for rent.

The manor house – which now houses a collection of splendid Arts and Crafts furniture – still has its Tudor Great Hall, a further Great Chamber with tapestries dating to 1700, some Tudor wall paintings and a beautiful early Georgian parlour. The terraced gardens – there are seven terraces in all – are filled with old roses, box hedges and beautifully clipped yews.

A Medieval Survival

The only major structural alterations in the house before the 20th century took place in the early 18th century; detailed records for this work still exist, which is how we know that the basic late medieval house was left unaltered. A little over a century later medieval houses were most unfashionable and the family deserted Owlpen for a nearby 1840s mansion, leaving it empty and decaying until Norman Jewson's arrival; this is why none of the contents we see today are original to the house. But the house itself is more than enough, with its rare architecture, its rich sense of the past and – of course – its ghost. Margaret of Anjou who slept here in 1471 is said to haunt the Great Chamber, dressed in cloak and wimple.

Outside in every direction beechwoods climb the steep-sided valley, and miles of woodland paths wander through a landscape rich in wildlife and plants and flowers.

Opposite: Nestling in a remote Gloucestershire valley, Owlpen Manor was rescued from dereliction by the Arts and Crafts Movement in the early 20th century. It is famous for its prominent yew trees and marvellous setting.

Below left: Owlpen has masses of beautiful decoration, particularly the ancient painted-cloth hangings. However, none of it is original to the house.

Below: The basic structure of the house, including many of the finest rooms, is medieval.

North of England

The country houses of the north of England reveal remarkable contrasts, between the classical elegance of a house like Chatsworth – once described as the National Gallery of the North – and remote, fortified manor houses such as Levens Hall, which began life as a massive square-built tower in a land where strength rather than style was the watchword. Away from these extremes, the north is also home to many of our most fascinating ancestral houses: Calke Abbey, for example, residence of the eccentric Harpur-Crewes; and, perhaps greatest of all, that monument to pride and ambition, Hardwick Hall, built by one of the most powerful women in Elizabethan England.

BELVOIR CASTLE

Belvoir (pronounced 'Beaver') Castle is a great survivor. Having been assaulted and partly or wholly demolished on several occasions – most notably during the Wars of the Roses and the English Civil War – it was rebuilt by John Webb, a pupil of Inigo Jones, in 1665–8, with further substantial work by James Wyatt at the end of the 18th century, only to succumb to a disastrous fire in 1816. This conflagration destroyed not only some of the furniture and pictures, but also much of the surviving late 17th-century house.

Right: The mock-medieval splendour of Belvoir dates largely from the 19th century, when it was rebuilt following a devastating fire.

Military Manoeuvres

Though Georgian, the current house has all the look and feel of a medieval castle – at least to the non-expert eye – with its yellow ironstone crenellations, towers and turrets.

The first of the four castles to stand on this site was built by William the Conqueror's standard bearer, Robert de Todeni, in the years immediately after the Norman Conquest. Robert was buried in the chapel of the priory he built next to his castle. When that early chapel was destroyed, Robert vanished, only to be rediscovered – still in his coffin – several centuries later during building work. His coffin is now in the castle itself.

When Robert de Todeni's last descendant died in the mid-13th century, the castle passed by marriage to the De Ros family. The last De Ros to own the castle was executed for supporting the Lancastrian side in the Wars of the Roses, and the castle passed to Lord Hastings, who used much of the stone and roofing lead to build his own castle at nearby Ashby-de-la-Zouch. When Henry VII came to the throne the political wheel turned full circle and the De Ros family got the castle back. One of their daughters married Sir Robert Manners; and the Manners family, who were awarded an earldom in 1525 and the dukedom of Rutland in 1703, still own the castle today.

Visitors to Belvoir first notice the amount of militaria on display – evidence of the family's long connection with soldiering in many arenas, including, as we have already

Previous page: Chatsworth House dominates the surrounding Derbyshire countryside.

seen, the English civil wars. When the family came out in support of the King, with the reluctant consent of the eighth earl (a moderate parliamentarian), Cromwell ordered the slighting – that is, the destruction – of the castle in 1649. Work began on the new castle almost immediately after the end of the Civil War and the building was complete by 1668.

Fire Damage

The fire of 1816 badly damaged much of the north and east wings, but Wyatt's south and west wings escaped relatively unscathed. The rebuilding work was overseen by Sir John Thoroton, the fifth duke's chaplain, who had worked with James Wyatt on the new building in 1801; and the Wyatt connection with the house continued when the great man's two sons Matthew and Benjamin redecorated the series of grand state rooms completed after the fire. The fifth duchess, a gifted amateur architect, is also said to have contributed substantially to the work carried out at this time.

Thoroton added the huge tower that projects from the west end of the north-east range of the house; at the east end the chapel can be identified by its neo-Gothic windows. Thoroton also created the Entrance Hall we see today and a staircase, both of which have a rather dark, sombre, almost forbidding air – perfect for a house that was designed to echo the romantic gloom of the medieval.

The house is curiously split in terms of building materials, with the north-west and

north-east sides of the house in grey stone as opposed to the warm yellow stone from which the rest of the house is constructed.

A Beautiful View

The house, known from about 1130 as Belvedere (meaning beautiful view), gets its name from the fact that it is sited on a hilltop which commands breathtaking views of what is otherwise a fairly flat landscape. In addition to the splendid grounds – parts of which have been beautifully restored by the present Duchess of Rutland – the house contains a number of magnificent paintings, most notably by Reynolds, Stubbs, Gainsborough and Poussin. The Poussins are currently on loan to the National Gallery until 2005 where they can be seen in the Poussin Room.

A tour of the house begins with the Entrance Hall or Guard Room, which has a curious room off to one side called the Speak and Word Room: here, by tradition, estate workers could come to talk privately and in person to the duke. Here, too, is a massive set of antlers: they are from the extinct Irish elk and were discovered deep in an Irish bog.

Opposite: *Antlers from the now-extinct Irish elk take pride of place in the entrance hall of Belvoir Castle, while leather buckets are on hand in case of fire, as are muskets in case of enemy attack.*

Left: *The Elizabeth Saloon by Matthew Wyatt is a sumptuous room where the ladies would withdraw to after dinner.*

Opposite: Wyatt's Gothic chapel. The painting of the Holy Family is by Bartolomé Murillo (1617–82).

Below: The grounds at Belvoir Castle are as enchanting as the house itself.

From the rib-vaulted Entrance Hall, stairs lead to the ballroom, rebuilt in the Early English Gothic style; here a model of the 17th-century house can be seen. Two chinoiserie-style rooms follow – a bedroom and a dressing room – before we reach the Elizabeth Saloon. This has a curiously over-decorated feel to it: a memorial to the fifth duchess, it is designed in what was, in the early 19th century, the new and highly fashionable Louis XIV style, and everywhere you look there are carvings, looking-glasses and silk hangings, nearly all in red and gold. The ceiling here was painted by Wyatt but in the style of Verrio, and there is a fine statue of the duchess herself.

Next comes the Dining Room, the work of Matthew Wyatt; of particular note here are the huge mahogany sideboards and the portrait of the fourth duke by Sir Joshua Reynolds.

Gainsborough and Holbein

The Picture Gallery, beautifully lit from above, has paintings by Jan Steen, Gainsborough

and a portrait of Henry VIII that has been attributed to Holbein.

The King's Rooms, named for George IV, were decorated in the mid-18th century Chinese style. From here the visitor takes the main staircase to the Regent's Gallery. Overlooking the wooded park and occupying two-thirds of the west wing, this was originally the most important room in the house. Originally the Long Gallery of the 17th-century house, it was remodelled by Wyatt and given a big bay window. Beautiful 18th-century Gobelin tapestries cover the walls and much of the furniture – including the fine boulle work – is in the French style.

Two libraries follow, both the work of Thoroton. The larger of the two, with its distinctive neo-Gothic windows, is only nominally a library: it was designed and has always been used as a book-filled reception room. Real study took place in the small adjoining library.

From the Regent's Gallery a staircase leads to Wyatt's Gothic chapel. Above the altar is a painting of the Holy Family by Murillo, and on the walls are three Mortlake tapestries based on the Raphael cartoons in the Victoria and Albert Museum. On the way back to the main staircase and entrance it is possible to visit the enormous, empty kitchen and pastry room which have been left as they were in the early 20th century.

Back to the Views

The views are without question the most impressive part of a visit to the gardens – on a clear day it seems as if one can see right across the county, and it is easy to understand why this hilltop among so much flat land appealed to the original castle builders.

The main aim of the gardeners today is to ensure that something is always in bloom, but if there is ever a lack of colour there are miles of paths and woodland walks to enjoy. Closer to hand, below the house, is the statue garden, containing a collection of beautiful 17th-century statues by Gabriel Caius Cibber, Charles II's court sculptor.

GRIMSTHORPE CASTLE

The history of Grimsthorpe Castle – a glorious mix of architectural styles – is matched in complexity only by the extraordinary history of the family who have owned the house since 1516. The family history is complex because the De Eresby title can descend direct through the female line, and has done so on a number of occasions. Add to this the fact that the family has accumulated quite a number of hereditary titles and you have a genealogy of intimidating intricacy.

Opposite: The Chinese Drawing Room still has its original hand-painted wallpaper.

Below: Grimsthorpe was largely rebuilt by the architect and playwright John Vanbrugh.

Ancient Origins

Grimsthorpe was first built in the 13th century and, though it has been modernized and refaced at various times, it has never quite been totally rebuilt. The 17th–18th-century playwright and architect John Vanbrugh is responsible for the present dominating baroque north front, but the south side of the house still shows the medieval tower alongside a Tudor façade. Inside, too, the house is quirky, in that it contains a number of items (particularly thrones and furnishings) from the old Houses of Parliament – the buildings engulfed by the fire of 1834 which almost entirely destroyed the old Palace of Westminster. These items came to the family through their hereditary role as Lord Great Chamberlain.

The Grimsthorpe estate is first recorded in 1192 when the De Gaunt family owned it. By the mid-14th century it had passed to Henry Lord Beaumont. It was the fifth Lord Beaumont who married Elizabeth Willoughby and began the family connection that lasts to this day. When the last of the Beaumonts died out, Henry VIII granted the reversion of the manor to

another William Willoughby who became 11th Baron Willoughby de Eresby when he married Maria de Salinas, a relative of Catherine of Aragon, in 1516.

A Child Bride

It was during Maria's lifetime and that of her daughter Katherine that much of the medieval house was rebuilt. Katherine was just six when her father died without a son, as a consequence of which the De Eresby title passed to Katherine and she became the 12th Baroness. Katherine married the Duke of Suffolk when she was just 14 and he 50; widowed in 1545, she lived abroad during the reign of Catholic Queen Mary, returning on the accession of Elizabeth.

By the time of Charles I, the 14th Baron de Eresby had inherited the title Lord Great Chamberlain and been created Earl of Lindsey. Lindsey, a staunch royalist, was killed during the Civil War along with two of his sons, but the family's fortunes revived at the Restoration and by the early 18th century Grimsthorpe was being modernized once again. It was now that Vanbrugh's north front

Below: Busts placed in high arcading give Grimsthorpe Castle's Great Hall a Romanesque feel.

Far below: Most of the decorative work dates to Vanbrugh's time, but earlier plasterwork survives in the chapel.

was added; however, more ambitious plans to remodel the whole house were cut back, which is why we are able to enjoy so many different architectural styles here today. By this time, the 18th baron was positively burdened down with honours, having also become Duke of Ancaster and Kesteven.

First Impressions

The first room visitors see today is the spectacularly imposing Vanbrugh Hall. The lofty room is enclosed on both east and west by two rows of arcades, one above the other at either side, leading to staircases (beneath the eastern staircase is an ancient low-vaulted hall). The arcades above the chimneypiece are filled with life-sized paintings of English kings by Sir James Thornhill, cleverly designed to look from a distance like statues.

Above the chimneypiece, which may well be the work of the great London church architect Nicholas Hawksmoor, is a cartouche with a monogram of George I as well as Willoughby de Eresby family crests.

At the top of the staircases, the ceilings of which are painted with splendid mythological scenes, we reach a landing with monumental doorcases based on those designed by Michelangelo at the Capitoline Palace in Rome. The first of the state rooms on this floor is the State Dining Room. Lit now by an imposing Venetian window, this may once have been the guard room in the Tudor house. The chimneypiece, carved with riding, fishing and sheep-shearing scenes, and the inlaid mahogany doors date to 1730. The room is hung with 17th-century Brussels tapestries showing

Below: *Arcading is a unique feature of Vanbrugh's Great Hall. Above the fireplace, which may well have been designed by Nicholas Hawksmoor, the blind arcades are filled with paintings designed to look like statues.*

Greek gods and a number of excellent portraits, including an unfinished picture by Sir Thomas Lawrence of Clementina Drummond, who married the 22nd Baron Willoughby de Eresby.

Here, too, are a walnut and gilt chair and footstool, both made for the Palace of Westminster; used by George III, they were traditionally the property of the Lord Great Chamberlain. The wall sconces in the shape of serpents were also accoutrements of the Lord Great Chamberlain's office and were brought here from the House of Lords.

The Tudor State Rooms

The King James room is decorated in typical 18th-century style but it is in fact the first of the original Tudor state rooms. The portrait of King James from which the room takes its name is by Paul van Somer and commemorates a visit by the king to the house. Most of the furniture is early 19th-century French and there is a pair of late 18th-century Boulle side tables. There is also a wonderful allegorical portrait, full of birds, fishes and distant landscape views, of Peregrine, the 13th Baron Willoughby de Eresby.

The State Drawing Room has an original Tudor oriel window and a series of large, impressive family and royal portraits. The South Corridor is hung with family portraits and contains the thrones of George IV, Queen Victoria and Edward VII as well as Queen Victoria's writing desk. More family portraits appear in the West Corridor; then we reach the Gothic Bedroom, dominated by its vast crimson bed covered with a bedspread worked by the Victorian 22nd Baron de Eresby.

Below: The King James Room, although Tudor in origin, is decorated in the typical early 18th-century fashion.

Despite its name, the Chinese Drawing Room is an extraordinary mix of Gothic, classical, rococo and Chinese styles; it has a beautiful coffered ceiling and original hand-painted blue Chinese wallpaper put up in 1811.

Beyond the House

The Chapel is in a surviving section of the late 17th-century house. The ceiling and plasterwork – elaborately detailed and very beautiful – date to this period, but much of the rest of this lofty room was refaced by Vanbrugh. Hugh Latimer, who was burned at the stake in 1555, preached here.

Before you leave the house, don't miss the extraordinary stone table held up by four grotesque figures, made in Henry VIII's time. Above it are the helmet and breastplate once worn by the 13th Baron de Eresby.

The gardens which look down on the lake are a mix of formal and informal, and include a topiary garden, a woodland garden and intricate parterres.

The house is now run by Jane Heathcote Drummond Willoughby, 28th Baroness Willoughby de Eresby, under the auspices of the Grimsthorpe and Drummond Castle Trust, a charitable body set up by her father, the third Earl of Ancaster.

Right: An elaborate double-flight staircase glimpsed through an archway in the Vanbrugh Hall.

NEWSTEAD ABBEY

Newstead Abbey, best known as the family home of the Romantic poet Lord Byron, was originally an Augustinian priory founded by Henry II in about 1170. In 1539, at the Dissolution of the Monasteries, Henry VIII granted Newstead to Sir John Byron for the then princely sum of £810. Sir John immediately converted the monastic buildings into a house. The house remained in the Byron family until the poet, seriously in debt and disgusted with what he saw as the narrow-minded hypocrisy of England, sold it in 1818 to Thomas Wildman, who had made his fortune from plantations worked by slaves in the West Indies.

A Gothic Masterpiece

Newstead's general layout and appearance are still recognizably monastic: Sir John Byron and his successors kept much of the original structure and layout, so that to this day the house retains its medieval character. The most famous medieval survivor is the west front of the church, dating from the late 13th century, with its statue of St Mary, to whom the priory was dedicated. The medieval chapter-house also survives.

The poet was the last in a string of Byrons to enjoy Newstead but spend nothing on its upkeep. Wildman, by contrast, spent a fortune repairing and preserving the house, employing the fashionable architect John Shaw to carry out the work. We have the early 19th-century passion for all things Gothic to thank for the fact that Shaw carefully blended his work with the original medieval structure.

The Wildman family was rich enough to fill the house with early furniture, pictures

Below: Newstead Abbey, set in the middle of Nottinghamshire parkland, was once the home of the Romantic poet Lord Byron.

and tapestries, but their tenure was to be relatively short: in 1861, Wildman's widow sold Newstead to the African explorer and friend of Sir David Livingstone, William Frederick Webb. When Webb died in 1899, the estate passed to his children and then to his grandson Charles Ian Fraser, who sold it to Sir Julien Cahn. Cahn, a famous local philanthropist, gave the house to Nottingham Corporation in 1931.

In Search of Byron

Today, most of those who visit Newstead come in search of the great Romantic poet, and the Newstead collection of objects associated with him is impressive: there are letters, portraits of Byron and his family and friends, as well as furniture and other personal effects, including most famously the poet's magnificent gilt-wood bed, brought here in 1808 by Byron himself from his student rooms in Cambridge.

Nevertheless, evidence of other owners is also plentiful. From the Wildman and Webb eras there is a great deal of splendid furniture, as well as paintings, letters, deeds and a series of Victorian photograph albums showing the house and gardens as they once were. There is also a unique collection of views of Newstead painted by the great Flemish artist Pieter Tillemans.

Newstead's Extensive Grounds

Newstead Abbey's beautiful 300-acre grounds are centred on the River Leen, which earlier gardeners used to create and feed a series of lakes and waterfalls. Archaeologists believe that some of the ponds were originally 'stew ponds' for the monastery: fishponds designed to ensure a ready supply of food for the monks. One such is the Eagle Pond which lies at the heart of the Great Garden, a

Left: The old cloisters were retained by the Byron family, so the house still has the feel of an abbey in places.

Opposite: The ceiling of the Great Drawing Room dates from 1631.

rare survival – in plan at least – of the late 17th-century walled and terraced formal garden to the east of the house.

Near the Eagle Pond is Byron's monument to his favourite dog, Boatswain, who died of rabies in 1808. In just the sort of gesture that marked him out as 'mad, bad and dangerous to know', the poet deliberately placed the monument where he calculated the high altar of the monastic church would have been!

Most of the other gardens around the house would not have been known to the poet, as they are mid- and late Victorian creations. The Fern Garden, Rockery, Sub-Tropical Garden, Spanish Garden and Japanese Garden were all created by Mrs William Frederick Webb or her daughters, Geraldine and Ethel, between 1861 and 1900. The Fern Garden was made for Mrs Webb between 1864 and 1865 and the Rockery, a miniature wilderness, was inspired by 'Venetia', a story by Benjamin Disraeli based on Newstead at the time when Byron was young. The Spanish Garden, on the site of the monastic burial ground, is a box-hedged parterre, while the wonderful herbaceous border in the Great Garden was created by the Webbs in about 1870. Recently restored, the 720-foot long border now provides a brilliant display throughout the summer.

Right: *Lord Byron brought this magnificent gilt-wood bed to Newstead Abbey in 1808, and it can be found in the tower where he slept.*

CALKE ABBEY

Most National Trust houses have a well-kept, beautifully restored (or repaired) look, but in recent years there have been moves towards trying to show houses – whether stately homes or smaller buildings – far more as they might have been at the time they were lived in. Calke Abbey, tucked away in a little-visited part of Derbyshire, is a classic example of the lived-in look.

An Extraordinary Family

Originally the site of a priory (hence its name), Calke Abbey – the second biggest house in Derbyshire – started its domestic life as a Tudor dwelling, but like so many big country houses it was updated in the 18th century. What makes it unique is the extraordinary family who owned it for centuries.

The Harpurs made their fortune as lawyers in the late 16th century, but subsequent generations were notoriously reclusive. Visitors to the house were discouraged while generation after generation inherited the house and parklands and, in the main, stayed put, living quietly at home. Over the years they amassed vast quantities of furniture, books, pictures, toys, carriages, wall hangings and collections of stuffed birds and eggs. Nothing was ever thrown away, so eventually all these accumulations filled not only the main rooms but all the storerooms, cupboards, corridors and even the attic.

Below: Elegant and remote, Calke Abbey provided a peaceful home for generations of reclusive Harpurs.

A Unique Acquisition

As a result, when the National Trust acquired the house in 1985, it found an interior unchanged since the 1880s, that high Victorian period when drawing rooms were packed with pictures and ornaments and bric-à-brac. In some rooms the clutter is almost overwhelming. With slightly flaky plaster, dust and rickety furniture, crowded passages and stairways, clocks and ornaments, the house looks as if a large family simply left it to its own devices. Perhaps the outstanding feature of the whole eccentric agglomeration is the huge collection of natural history specimens, the lifetime's work of a Victorian owner, Sir Vauncey Harpur-Crewe.

When the Trust began to catalogue the items in the house it also found – still in its packing case – a complete and magnificent 18th-century state bed. Uniquely – because it had always been kept under wraps – none of the gorgeous hangings for the bed had ever been exposed to the light, so they had not faded. It is a glimpse – more authentic than most – into a vanished world.

Below: The Bird Lobby houses Sir Vauncey's large collection of stuffed birds. Calke Abbey is full of the weird and the wonderful.

HARDWICK HALL

Hardwick Hall is, if you like, a show-off's house – everything about it proclaims the wealth and importance of its originator, the remarkable Bess of Hardwick. The house dominates the landscape for miles around. Vast and imposing, it has far more and bigger windows than any comparable house and, hence, more glass: glass was expensive and so a conspicuous sign of wealth, and Bess was determined to have as much of it as possible.

Bess of Hardwick

Bess, who became enormously wealthy through her marriages, built a number of houses, but Hardwick was her pride and joy. It was finished in 1597 and is still an extraordinary monument to a woman who began life in far from aristocratic circumstances. Elizabeth, Dowager Countess of Shrewsbury – she had been widowed four times by the time she embarked on Hardwick Hall – was born in 1527 in a medieval house on the site of the present hall. Her family had been reasonably prosperous farmers in the area since at least the 13th century, but socially they were no higher than gentry. She never knew her father, who died before she was a year old. At 13 she was married to Robert Barlow, a cousin, but her young husband died soon after the marriage and, since he was not of

Below: The west elevation of Hardwick Hall is a sea of glass, which is a reflection of the wealth and status of its founder, Bess of Hardwick.

age, he left her nothing. She then became a lady in waiting at court, one of the army of genteel young women hired to attend on ladies of noble birth. Here she met Sir William Cavendish, one of Henry VIII's royal commissioners appointed to dissolve the monasteries; and it was Bess's eventual marriage to Sir William, 22 years her senior, that set her on the road to wealth and influence. The couple had eight children, six of whom survived, and it was from this union, too, that the Cavendishes – later dukes of Devonshire – were descended.

A Shrewd Shrewsbury

Sir William bought Chatsworth House (see pages 152–57) for Bess, along with a number of other houses. When he died, Bess

was still young, hugely wealthy and – by now – shrewd enough to know that her best bet would be to marry again and to marry well. Her third husband, from 1559, was Sir William St Loe, another elderly and very wealthy man. Five years later he, too, died, leaving Bess his fortune. It was then that she made her last and most powerful marriage: in 1567, to George Talbot, sixth Earl of Shrewsbury. It was not, in the end at least, a happy marriage – Shrewsbury called her that 'sharp bitter shrew' – and Bess saw little of him, partly because they simply didn't get on and partly because he spent 15 years guarding Mary, Queen of Scots before her execution. By 1584, the couple were no longer living together and Bess, still with her own huge personal fortune, bought

Below: The High Great Chamber has to be one of the finest rooms anywhere in Europe. It still has its original painted plaster frieze illustrating the Hunt of Diana, below which are Brussel tapestries depicting the great Greek legend of Ulysses; the tapestries were brought to the house by Bess herself.

Hardwick from her brother, who had huge debts. When Shrewsbury died in 1590, Bess conceived the idea for the magnificent house we know today.

Smythson's Symmetry

Bess commissioned the local architect and builder Robert Smythson to carry out the work. With its extraordinary vast windows that shine along all four storeys, the house (famously described as 'more glass than wall') is wonderfully symmetrical. Each tower is decorated with Elizabeth's initials carved in stone. She chose ES – Elizabeth Shrewsbury – for Shrewsbury was the title of which she was most proud.

Among the most striking original internal features is the magnificent plasterwork of the ornate ceilings, which reach their high point in the painted plaster frieze in the High Great Chamber. Much of the furniture was brought here from Chatsworth in the 19th century, but the tapestries and embroidery have almost certainly been here since Bess's time.

Outside can be seen the remains of Hardwick Old Hall, the house where Bess was born, and there are beautiful walled courtyards and gardens as well as orchards and a herb garden. The parkland surrounding the house now provides a home for numerous rare breeds of cattle and sheep.

Bess was buried in what is now Derby Cathedral. A life-sized effigy commissioned in her memory shows that, for all her drive and ambition, Bess was just 5 feet 3 inches tall.

Below: *Both the Long Gallery and the High Great Chamber have wonderfully high ceilings. The Long Gallery is filled with light, thanks to Smythson's vast windows, and 81 portraits line the walls.*

CHATSWORTH

From the day it was built, Chatsworth was on the tourist trail. The newly emerging middle classes of the 18th century, including the potter Josiah Wedgwood, came here to see what was already talked about as the palace of the north. A typical tour of the time would include the Derbyshire caves, the Wilds of the Peaks, a quick visit to a coal pit – and then Chatsworth.

Below: *Vast and imposing, Chatsworth has more than 8,000 panes of glass and is surrounded by fantastic gardens landscaped by Capability Brown.*

Opposite: *The gallery includes work by sculptor Antonio Canova.*

The Cavendish Legacy

The Chatsworth estate was originally owned by the Agard family. Then, in 1549, the estate was bought by Sir William Cavendish, whose Suffolk-based family – like so many others – had amassed great wealth from church lands given to them by Henry VIII. Cavendish set about building a house on his new estate, but when he died eight years later it was still unfinished. The work was completed by Sir William's widow Elizabeth, Bess of Hardwick, who also famously built Hardwick Hall some 15 miles away (see pages 149–51).

By 1618, the Cavendishes had made remarkable progress from gentry to nobility: Bess's son William, who had bought the estate from his elder brother, was now Earl of Devonshire. His three-storey Elizabethan courtyard house was to last less than a hundred years, for very little of the interior structure of the old house was kept when rebuilding began in 1686 for the fourth earl, and the external appearance of the house changed out of all recognition as enthusiasm for classical design had by now entirely superseded any attachment to the English vernacular.

William Talman designed the south and east fronts, Thomas Archer the north. The earl (from 1694, the first Duke of Devonshire) may well have designed the

Above: The beauty of Chatwsorth is that it does not suffer from quantity above quality. There is a huge amount of decorative work, including these superb leather wall coverings, but it is all of the highest standard.

Opposite: This Dining Room was the work of Wyatt in the 18th century. It has a wealth of paintings, including Gainsborough's portrait of Georgiana, Duchess of Devonshire, and a magnificent fireplace flanked by life-sized figures.

complete the painted walls and ceiling, which show scenes from the life of Christ, while Samuel Watson designed and executed the alabaster altar. The panelling is of cedar, a pungent wood that still exudes a faint aroma. The chairs and giant brass candlesticks date from the 17th century.

A Veritable Art Gallery

It would take a full-length book to do justice to the vast collection of paintings and sculpture at Chatsworth; again, it must suffice here to pick out just a few pieces of particular interest. Among the best early works is the first-century Roman mother-and-child sculpture in the North Entrance Hall. A wonderful portrait by Henry Briggs of the Chatsworth gardener (and later designer of the Crystal Palace) Joseph Paxton, who created spectacular waterworks, greenhouses and rock gardens in the 19th century, can be found in the Leicester Corridor; and there is an extraordinary trompe l'œil painting of a violin in the State Music Room.

In the West Sketch Gallery hang numerous pictures of various Cavendish ancestors by Reynolds, Sargent, Kneller, Millais and a host of others. The Great Dining Room in the north wing contains a number of exquisite 18th-century vases made from bluejohn – a semi-precious stone found only in Derbyshire, which is very difficult to work and was first used in pottery by Wedgwood. On the walls are no fewer than seven works by van Dyck. In the adjacent Sculpture Gallery, as well as famous sculptures by Canova, there are pictures by Sir Edwin Landseer and Frans Hals, and even a Rembrandt.

Among the oddities at Chatsworth are a giant ancient Greek marble foot, a lace cravat carved from wood, the fan of a Rolls-Royce jet engine and four royal thrones.

The Chatsworth estate extends to some 35,000 acres – land held right across Derbyshire and Staffordshire – and includes a mixture of woodlands, farms, rivers and even whole villages. The Hunting Tower on the hill above the house dates from the 1580s. There are lakeside walks in the 1,000 acres of parkland; a cascade created in 1694 is still there, along with a dome-topped temple. Queen Mary's Bower is the only part of the garden design that survives from the 16th century. Visitors can also examine an excavated coal tunnel!

The 11th duke, who died in 2004, admitted that when he was a child he found it easy to get lost in the huge house despite having lived there all his life. This is perhaps no surprise when one considers the following extraordinary statistics: Chatsworth has 17 staircases, 3,426 feet of corridors and passageways, more than 2,000 light fittings, nearly 8,000 panes of glass, 56 lavatories and 359 doors!

The Dowager Duchess of Devonshire is the last of the glamorous Mitford sisters who took interwar society by storm. Her family were notoriously talented and eccentric, a tradition she continues: she recently published a cookery book in which she confessed to not having cooked a thing for over 40 years.

Lyme Park

Lyme, one of the biggest and most impressive country houses in Cheshire, is a curious mix: on the outside it looks exactly like an Italian palace, its design heavily influenced by the ideas of Palladio; on the inside its Tudor origins are clear. Much of the interior and all the present exterior is the work of the Italian architect Giacomo Leoni.

An Ancestral Home

Lyme has been the home of the Legh family for some 600 years. The story begins in 1398 when Margaret Legh received the house in exchange for an annuity she had inherited from her grandfather, who in turn had received the annual payment from Edward the Black Prince as a reward for fighting the French at the Battle of Crécy.

What was probably a small house or hunting lodge began its transformation in the 1500s when Sir Piers Legh enlarged and modernized it. Successive generations continued to add and embellish, but the major alterations came in the 1720s with the arrival of Leoni. Given what amounted to a free hand, this enormously fashionable Venetian architect built new façades (but encasing rather than demolishing the old walls), knocked many of the old small rooms into the spaces that now exist, and embellished the interior throughout with that period's most fashionable style of decoration – the vastly elaborate rococo. Leoni also built the superb courtyard we see today.

Refurbishment and Restoration

Once the house had been modernized it was felt that the collections of furniture and pictures had to be changed too, and in the middle of the 18th century Peter Legh began to collect the magnificent furniture the house still contains. But towards the end of the 18th century and into the 19th the house was neglected. When Thomas Legh came of age in November 1813, he began a

Left: The Dutch Garden to the south-west of the house is actually a sunken Italian garden.

Below: Fit for a king: the beautifully prepared dining table at Lyme Park.

Below: The Long Gallery is
one of Lyme Park's earliest
rooms, although the ceiling is
the work of an estate carpenter,
completed in 1926.

programme of restoration that also involved more alteration. He employed the then fashionable architect Lewis Wyatt to carry out the work, but Wyatt had the sense to leave the best 17th- and 18th-century rooms relatively untouched.

The series of state rooms is the most immediately impressive, particularly the Saloon with its wonderful rococo ceiling and carved limewood decorations on the walls – all said to be by Grinling Gibbons. More carved wood around the chimney glass is contemporary with Gibbons' work but of lesser quality. The ceiling in the Saloon is of a later date than the carving and was probably embellished by Wyatt. The Dining Room is the only other state room where Gibbons' carvings appear – in a panel over the fireplace.

The state rooms also contain family portraits, 18th-century furniture and, in the Entrance Hall, a magnificent collection of Mortlake tapestries dating from 1625 to 1636 and showing scenes from the story of Hero and Leander. There is also a fascinating collection of clocks, all by English makers. The clocks – mostly examples of longcase and bracket clocks – include some real rarities, especially the examples by Tompion and Knibb. Among a collection of beautiful 18th- and 19th-century glass there are six Jacobite toasting glasses.

Below: The Long Gallery is one of Lyme Park's earliest rooms, although the ceiling is the work of an estate carpenter, completed in 1926.

Garden Variety

Lyme boasts a lovely Edwardian rose garden, a parterre, a Victorian garden, a ravine garden and Wyatt's wonderful early Victorian conservatory, known as the Orangery and used as such. There are herbaceous borders, a rhododendron walk, mixed borders to the terraces and also a reflection lake. Confusingly, what is called the Dutch Garden is actually a sunken Italian garden. A true Dutch garden did exist in the 18th century, in the area then known as the Old Garden, but was swept away by Wyatt's alterations. William Legh (who in 1892 became the first Lord Newton) re-established the Dutch Garden in the 1860s,

and the results of his efforts are what we see today.

The design of the various component gardens means something is in blossom at virtually all times of the year. Another exterior feature worth attention is the Cage, an 18th century hunting tower.

By the 1940s, when the third Lord Newton inherited the house, the costs of running it were vast and in 1946 he gave Lyme to the National Trust. Today Lyme Park retains most of its original parkland and estate, running to just under 1,400 acres, and much of this almost certainly looks just as it did when it was a medieval deer park.

Below: The Saloon, with its 1730s rococo ceiling and carved limewood decoration – a mixture of the work of Leoni and Wyatt – is enhanced by a chandelier dating from the reign of George II and a fireplace installed by James Wyatt.

ASTLEY HALL

The front of Astley Hall, with its great glass windows, is designed to make us sit up and take note. Though not on the scale of the 'wall of glass' at Hardwick Hall, it is none the less impressive. Of course, plenty of glass would not only advertise the builder's wealth, but would also fill what might otherwise have been a dark house with light at a time when most houses were rather dark and dingy inside.

Below: *Elizabethan Astley Hall from the gardens; the long gallery of continuous glazing is a very unusual feature. This site has been occupied since the Bronze Age.*

A False Façade
The front of Astley Hall is of brick (rendered to look like stone in the late 18th or early 19th century), another expensive building material designed to impress. It was probably built in the 1650s or 1660s, but it conceals an earlier timber-framed house which was built in Elizabethan times, probably as

early as 1580. Archaeological evidence suggests the site of Astley Hall has been inhabited since the Bronze Age, and recent archaeological work has uncovered evidence of medieval occupation.

The first recorded occupiers of the hall are the Charnocks, who lived here from the late 1570s until 1653. The family,

Left: *Some of the plasterwork figures at Astley Hall were so large they had to be moulded on wooden frames before being attached to the ceiling.*

landowners of the squirearchy class, came from a village called Charnock Richard, from which they took their own name. Having acquired Astley Hall, Robert Charnock set about rebuilding the medieval house. We know that Robert married Isobel Norris of Speke Hall, Liverpool, and after her death he was to marry four more times. The Charnocks were also implicated in at least one of Mary, Queen of Scots' plots to oust her sister Elizabeth from the throne: Robert's brother John Charnock was eventually executed for his involvement in what came to be known as the Babington Plot.

Handed Down the Generations

After Robert's death in 1616, Astley passed to his son Thomas, who became an MP in 1624. Thomas's son, another Robert, fought on the side of the royalists during the Civil War and was badly injured. When he died in 1653, the estate passed to his daughter Margaret, who married Richard Brooke; the couple had 12 children, and though Richard died in 1712, astonishingly Margaret lived to be 99, dying in 1744. It was during this

couple's early days at Astley that the glass front was built and the magnificent Drawing Room and Great Hall ceilings added. The formal gardens to the front of the house also date from this period.

The last of the Brookes – Peter – died in 1787, and in the absence of an heir the house passed to Susannah, Peter's sister. Susannah, who married twice, survived to be 90. On dying in 1852, the house went to her son Robert Townley Parker, MP for Preston, whose son Thomas inherited it in his turn. When Thomas died in 1906 without children the house passed to a nephew, Reginald Tatton. In 1922, Reginald donated the hall to the local council, which has owned it ever since, together with the surrounding parkland. The council (then Chorley Corporation) converted the bedrooms in the east wing into an art gallery and the Astley Hall Museum and Art Gallery opened in 1924.

The Long Gallery

The long gallery was a vital room in any Elizabethan house with the slightest pretensions to gentility. It was the room

Right: The extraordinarily voluptuous plaster ceiling in the drawing room bears down heavily on a space which is already crowded with Flemish tapestries.

where the family – through portraits and possessions – was, as it were, on show, although there is evidence that long galleries also provided a place for the family to play and exercise during periods of bad weather. The Long Gallery at Astley runs the full length of the south front. On three sides the walls shimmer with the vast windows that take up most of the space where the walls would normally be; most of the glass is original and dates to the early 1600s. The huge 27-foot-long shuffleboard table reminds us of the gallery's role as a room for play – it also reminds us that shuffleboard (also called shovel board) was one of England's most popular games in the 16th and 17th centuries.

As with the Long Gallery, the Oak Room benefits from large amounts of glass – in this case arranged in two long ranges. The Cromwell Bed (which may have been slept in by the parliamentary leader) is very much the centrepiece: with its floral panels on the headboard, matched by designs on a later washstand in the same room, it is typical of the solid oak tester beds of the late 17th century.

An Elizabethan Gem

The Cromwell Room is one of the least altered rooms in the house and appears now as it would have done when the Elizabethan house was completed in 1580. The fireplace certainly dates from this time, as do the ceiling and panelling. The room gets its name from the legend – and it is probably no more than that – that Cromwell stayed here in 1648, but the bed – known as the Charnock Bed – has the Charnock coat of arms on the headboard.

A door leads to the Stucco Room, which has a hiding place concealed behind the wall at the side of the fireplace: the Charnocks were Catholics and they may well have hidden co-religionists and priests who had fallen foul of the Protestant authorities. The room gets its name from what look like fine plasterwork panels and carved heads – which is odd, as what looks like plasterwork is almost certainly timber painted to look like plaster.

Above: The decorative plasterwork is of the highest quality but we know nothing of the craftsmen who carried out the work.

Opposite: The Great Hall is central to the design of Astley, and the flooring, ceiling and panelling have survived unchanged for more than three centuries.

Central to the design of Astley Hall is the Great Hall with its extraordinary plasterwork ceiling, some of the figures on which are so large that they had to be moulded on timber frames and only then attached to the ceiling. There is evidence to suggest that much of the ceiling work was made for another house and then brought here. Stylistically the ceiling shows Italian influences, but we do not know the names of the craftsmen.

The East Wing

From the Great Hall a small anteroom leads to the Library (also known as the Inlaid Room) and the Dining Room. Both these rooms are in the east wing, the later, Georgian part of the house. Completed in 1825, the Library has late 16th-century inlaid oak panelling and some fine Elizabethan oak furniture.

The Dining Room, also designed in the 1820s, has floor-to-ceiling windows giving views out across the garden; one window has a flight of steps to allow diners to take a stroll after they have eaten.

By the end of the 18th century, fashions had changed and dining or sitting in a room as big as the Great Hall would no longer have been socially acceptable, custom now demanding a more intimate setting for greeting and entertaining friends. The Drawing Room admirably fulfilled this purpose – and still reflected the splendours of the Great Hall, boasting a ceiling contemporary with that in the larger room that may indeed have been executed by the same craftsmen. The Drawing Room also has a collection of beautiful walnut and rosewood furniture and a set of superb 17th-century Brussels tapestries showing the story of Jason and the Golden Fleece.

The Working Heart

The kitchen has a fascinating charcoal stove which was probably installed in the late 18th century, but many of the kitchen implements – pestle and mortar, cauldrons, pots and so on – are at least a century older. The nearby scullery has a slipper bath that would have been hauled up the stairs to the bedrooms of various members of the family.

The north wing was divided into servants' rooms – probably in the 19th century – but some of the timbers here still bear the Elizabethan carpenters' marks. Two sets of servants' staircases lead up from the tiny passage here, with the aim of keeping to the absolute minimum the chances of the servants meeting the family or their guests in passing.

Astley Hall was once surrounded by formal gardens of the sort much loved by the Elizabethans, but like so many gardens it succumbed to the pressures of the 18th-century picturesque fashion and the subsequent Romantic movement. The stables (built in the late 18th century) and walled kitchen garden remain to remind us that a house like this would have been a virtually self-sufficient community at a time when the roads were bad and horses the only form of transport.

HAREWOOD HOUSE

Harewood started life as a castle built to guard a ford over the River Wharfe from the wild men of Northumberland and beyond. The castle was certainly complete by the early 1100s and formed part of that vast and remarkable network of Norman castles designed to keep the local population – whether in Sussex or Cheshire, Northumberland or Wales – in awe of their new masters.

Below: *A picture of elegance, Harewood was designed by John Carr in the mid-18th century and this front was Italianized by Sir Charles Barry in the mid-19th century.*

Adam's Student

Over the next few centuries the castle passed through a number of families including the Aldburghs, the Gascoignes, the Wentworths and the Boulters. At least one former owner – the Earl of Strafford – was beheaded for treason. The Lascelles family, from whom the present earl is descended, bought the estate relatively recently, in 1738.

The Lascelles were an old Yorkshire family of Norman descent but by the 18th century most of their money came from slave plantations in the West Indies – money enough to build the present house, which was completed in 1772. The main architect was John Carr of York, but his plans were studied and approved by Robert Adam.

The fields that surrounded the new house were quickly landscaped by Lancelot 'Capability' Brown in the usual 18th-century picturesque style: a lake surrounded by natural-looking groups of trees in the manner of a Poussin or Lancret landscape. Thousands of tons of soil were moved to create the right slopes in the right places; streams were dammed, trees planted.

Thomas Chippendale was brought to the house to design furniture specifically for the hundreds of new rooms, and over the succeeding years vast collections of paintings, pieces of furniture and works of art were amassed and augmented.

The Earls' Changes

By 1812, the Lascelles family had become earls of Harewood and, in keeping with the family's new status, Harewood House was greatly altered. Charles Barry (1795–1860), the architect of the new Houses of Parliament, removed the classical portico on the south side of the house and added a rather heavy terrace and a third floor, transforming what had been a big house into something closer to a palace.

Over the past 50 years, Victorian design has been regarded generally with some distaste compared to the more delicate features of 18th-century interior decoration, and, accordingly, the great Adam interiors at Harewood have been meticulously restored.

Adamesque Harewood

The first part of the house the visitor reaches is the Entrance Hall, one of the best Adam rooms in the house. It is now dominated by a magnificent alabaster carving of *Adam* (the first man) by the sculptor Jacob Epstein. This is the only 20th-century note in a room that is in other respects entirely the work of the 18th-century Adam, with its delicate plaster friezes, ceiling, and painted Chippendale chairs – chairs, it might be added, that were designed for show rather than use: they are not, apparently, sturdy enough to sit on!

Green, white and grey are the dominant colours in the Old Library (layers of old paint were removed to reveal the original colour scheme); here again there are Chippendale chairs, as well as a beautiful 18th-century clock.

The China Room gets its name from the magnificent collection of Sèvres porcelain

Above: The Gallery, with its collection of Old Masters paintings, runs the full length of the west side of the house. The ceiling was designed by Robert Adam.

Below: The bedrooms are rich in delicate furniture and Adam ceilings and decoration.

Opposite: The drawing rooms are filled with magnificent paintings and china, and all the furniture is by Thomas Chippendale.

housed here, while Princess Mary's Dressing Room is delightfully intimate, with a fireplace in a curving recess and decorated throughout in the usual Adam style. The room now houses one or two early family portraits.

Scenes and Silks

The East Bedroom has a sunflower ceiling, Dutch and English pictures, and more furniture by Chippendale. The Watercolour Room includes pictures by some of the greatest British watercolourists – two, one each by J.M.W. Turner and Thomas Girtin, are particularly special as they depict scenes at Harewood. Girtin died young, and Turner said of him: 'If Girtin had lived I'd have starved.'

Less obviously Adam-inspired, Lord Harewood's Sitting Room contains more modern pictures, including several by 20th-century artists Walter Sickert and John Piper.

The State Bedroom and its extraordinarily lavish Chippendale State Bed were

kept for visiting royalty, although by the early 20th century the Lascelles were part of the royal family anyway – the sixth earl having married Princess Mary, the Princess Royal. The green silk walls, though modern, reflect the original colour scheme.

A Bookish Family

The Spanish Library was originally a dressing room, but it is a now a very grand library indeed. Designed by Charles Barry, it is also rather dark and decidedly Victorian-looking. The Lascelles were clearly a bookish family, for after the Spanish Library comes the Library proper, a high-ceilinged and High Victorian room with grand mahogany bookcases (again by Barry) and a beautiful Adam overmantel.

The portrait-filled Yellow and Cinnamon Drawing Rooms follow, decorated to reflect the dominant Adam colour scheme; then comes the Gallery, which runs the whole length of the west side of the house. Its Adam ceiling is a fascinating mix of oblongs, crosses, ovals and octagons; its windows,

Above: *The lavish State Bedroom was reserved for visiting royalty, and has been wonderfully restored to its original 18th-century style with care and attention.*

large and light-filled, are flanked by pillars. There is rare china here, as well as Chippendale mirrors and some of the best pictures in the house: portraits by Veronese, Bellini and Titian, among others.

The final two rooms open to the public (the family still live in part of the house) offer a striking contrast: the Dining Room is entirely Victorian while the Music Room is the least altered Adam room in the house.

The grounds are kept much as Capability Brown planned them, with broad vistas and strategically planted clumps of trees. There is a later terrace by Barry, however, as well as a modern bird garden which helps conserve up to 120 exotic bird species, many of which are rare or endangered in the wild.

CASTLE HOWARD

Not a fortified stronghold, rather a grand house, yet Castle Howard has the distinction of having taken more than a century to complete. Much of its fame today stems from the part it played in the television adaptation of Evelyn Waugh's novel Brideshead Revisited *in the 1980s; but Castle Howard's history began when the third Earl of Carlisle decided, towards the end of the 17th century, that he needed a new house. He asked the leading architect of the day, William Talman, to produce plans, but when they were ready the earl rejected them out of hand. Sir John Vanbrugh – already a well-known playwright and a friend of the earl's – then produced a plan that was accepted, which was remarkable given that Vanbrugh had no architectural experience at that time.*

A Complex Design

It took three years just to agree the plans, but there were still surprises in store: initially, two wings were designed to lead away from an imposing central block, but the huge dome that eventually appeared was something of an afterthought, added to the design after building had begun in 1699.

Ten years later the basic shape of the house was complete, with the exception of the west wing. It was adorned with seahorse carvings, cherubs, coronets and ciphers as well as a magnificent carving of Diana. Both Doric and Corinthian columns were used (on different façades), and the whole house literally bristled with statues, urns and carvings. Much of the lavish interior had also been completed. But of the west wing only the front was in place, and it was to be many years before the wing was completed. In fact,

Below: *Castle Howard is imposing, if a little lopsided – the dome, seen here from the garden elevation, was an afterthought.*

Opposite: *The Great Hall is Castle Howard's baroque masterpiece – a whirlwind of arches, balconies, and columns.*

Below: *The dome was restored after a disastrous fire broke out in the house in 1940.*

not until 1841 was the west wing fully decorated. Both the third and fourth earls were dead by then, and the finished wing bore no relation to the original design. It had been completed by Thomas Robinson in a Palladian style which was so out of kilter with the rest of the house that it infuriated subsequent owners.

Charmingly Lopsided

Work continued on and off until, in the late 19th century, the two pavilions on the ends of each wing were removed in a desperate attempt to make the house more symmetrical; but even today it presents a rather lopsided if endearing appearance. A difficult situation was made far worse when

fire destroyed 20 rooms and the whole dome in 1940. Only in 1960 was the decision taken to repair the damage.

Today, the house offers the visitor a magnificent collection of china – including examples of early Crown Derby and Meissen – and paintings by Canaletto, Rubens, Holbein and Gainsborough. There are also a gigantic bog oak and silver-gilt wine cooler, as well as, in the Chapel, an embroidered screen by the great pioneer of the 19th-century Arts and Crafts movement, William Morris.

The gardens include two lakes, and several temples and follies are scattered here and there throughout the estate – the Pyramid and the Seventh Earl Monument, among others.

BURTON AGNES HALL

There has been a house at Burton Agnes since 1173, and the original manor house is still there, with Sir Henry Griffiths' early 17th-century house in front of it. Remarkably, despite the fact that the estate has passed through the female line on several occasions, it has never been sold.

Below: Red brick with stone quoins, Burton Agnes Hall is the only home designed by the Elizabethan architect Robert Smythson for which the original plans survive.

Passed Down the Female Line

The house takes its name from one of Roger de Stuteville's daughters, Anne, who would certainly still recognize the Lower Chamber, as the surviving Norman room. Above this room is the early 17th-century house, behind which is the original manor house, also open to the public.

By 1600, Burton Agnes had passed through another daughter into the hands of the Griffith family. Sir Henry Griffiths then employed the architect Robert Smythson to rebuild the house. Smythson was Elizabeth I's master mason, responsible for, among others, Longleat and Hardwick Hall, but Burton Agnes is the only house he built for which the original plans survive.

Red brick with stone quoins, the house has all the beauty of an era which retained English architectural traditions while embracing in part newly fashionable continental forms.

The Gatehouse is a splendid piece of architecture with its grand symmetry and dome-topped angle turrets. Placed centrally in a large panel above the route through the gateway are the arms of James I with, on either side, draped female figures or caryatids.

An Eccentric Design

Smythson made the entrance front south-facing and tucked the front door into the

side of one of the bays. Viewed from the east, the house is delightfully eccentric in shape, with the front appearing to be higher than the back sections. This is no trick of the light: the front is indeed higher – it had to be in order to allow space for the fashionable Long Gallery.

If the date above the door is to be believed, Burton Agnes was completed in 1601, but another date – 1610 – carved into the south-east bedroom frieze may be closer to the actual date of completion. Above the front door one can also see the family coats of arms – those of the Griffiths family and the later Throckmortons are included, as well as Queen Elizabeth's arms. A bowling green that ran between the Gatehouse and the main building was removed in Victorian times and replaced with the yew trees and lawn we see today.

Visitors first enter the Great Hall with its magnificent timber and plaster screen, carved with knights and ladies, apostles and angels; the intricacy and quality of the woodcarving is matched by the fine plasterwork and panelling. The long oak table is almost certainly contemporary with the screen. On the huge chimneypiece there are carvings in alabaster of the wise and foolish virgins – the latter singing and dancing, the former washing and sewing. Above the fireplace are the carved wooden arms of Sir Thomas Boynton; the Boyntons were another family that inherited the house through the female line. There is a pair of Francis Cotes portraits of Sir Griffith Boynton, and his wife. Other notable paintings are of Charles II and James II.

The Inner Hall has a superb portrait by Gerhardts of three of the daughters of the man who built Burton Agnes and also a splendid parquetry chest known as a Nonesuch Chest – named after the great but long vanished palace of that name.

Angels and Devils

The Red Drawing Room has an elaborate Elizabethan chimneypiece, the central carving on which depicts the Dance of Death: a skeleton capers on earthly vanities in the form of weapons, sceptres and a mitre. The chimney also shows the good going into the arms of the angels while the bad are warmly greeted by the devil himself. The panelling here is gilded and there is a collection of 18th-century porcelain.

The Chinese Room has lacquer panelled walls, an 18th-century chimneypiece, a late

Below left: *Elegant grounds surround the house.*

Below: *The Norman Room sits beneath the 17th-century structure.*

Georgian chandelier and a good portrait of another Sir Griffith Boynton by Philippe Mercier.

Faith, Hope and Charity

The Dining Room, which strikes one as rather plain after the Chinese Room, has a magnificent fireplace that was once in the Long Gallery; central to the carved design are the figures of Faith, Hope and Charity. The chairs here are by Chippendale and there is a rare silver race cup in the centre of the table. The room contains a number of 18th-century landscapes, including a good Gainsborough painting of Bath and a portrait of Burton Agnes Hall itself. There is a famous portrait of Oliver Cromwell by Robert Walker, a Joshua Reynolds and a rather poignant little study of Peregrine, the only son of Sir Matthew Boynton, the first baronet, possibly by Lely. Peregrine died at the age of just five.

The staircase is a masterpiece of Elizabethan carving and at the top of the

Opposite: The Great Hall has an extraordinary plaster and timber screen and a similarly impressive alabaster fireplace.

Above: This simple painting of boys going fishing contrasts with many of the grander, more imposing portraits in the house.

Right: The staircase at Burton Agnes Hall is a masterpiece of Elizabethan carving.

stairs there are a number of family portraits.

The Queen's State Bedroom has the most complex and arguably the most beautiful ceiling in the house – a mass of honeysuckle, oak, holly and thistle motifs. The chimney-piece is carved with allegorical figures and, hidden among the beautiful carvings, the precise date the work was completed: July 12, 1610. This room is also believed to be haunted by the ghost of Katherine Griffiths, the daughter of the man who built the house.

The Long Gallery, which gives the house its irregular shape, was divided into servants' bedrooms in the early 19th century, but it was partly restored in the 1950s and then fully restored to its total length in 1974.

The Library is another 1950s restoration, but it is filled with beautiful 18th-century furniture, including a fine Sheraton bureau-cabinet.

The Old Walled Garden was restored in the late 1980s; there is also a maze, a jungle garden and a knot garden. The house itself is surrounded by lawns, yews, ponds and fountains.

Above: The Queen's Bedroom has an incredibly ornate plasterwork ceiling and is one of the most luxurious state rooms of Burton Agnes Hall.

Right: Splendid lacquer panels and a late Georgian chandelier grace the Chinese Room.

LEVENS HALL

The De Redman family built the first house at Levens in about 1350. At the time, this part of the north of England was regularly raided by warlike tribes from Northumberland, the border country and Scotland, and records suggest the first house was simply a pele tower – a small defensive fortification. The family would have lived in the upper stories while their animals were kept below. By the later 16th century, the tower house had become the property of the Bellingham family, who used the old tower as the centrepiece for their new mansion. Much of the house we see today is the house the Bellinghams built.

Jacobean Furnishings

Roughly a century later, in 1694, Levens had become the property of Colonel James Grahame. Grahame left the main house almost unchanged, but added a wing at the back and brought a great deal of Jacobean oak and other furniture here, much of which remains to this day. The last major phase of work at Levens was the construction of the Howard Tower, completed in 1820.

Apart from its antiquity and beautiful setting, Levens today is a special place for many reasons. The Dining Room is one of the highlights, with its extraordinary and

Below: The Dining Room at Levens Hall has beautiful embossed Cordoban leather wall coverings.

now very rare embossed Cordoban leather wall coverings.

Levens also contains an example of English patchwork (a craft rather like quilting but using scraps of second-hand material) from 1708, as well as a number of good paintings. Levens has connections with both the Duke of Wellington and Admiral Lord Nelson, and visitors can see a number of items associated with both men.

Beaumont's Gardens

The beautiful Topiary Gardens for which the house is justly famous survive from the 1690s when Guillaume Beaumont, who had worked at Versailles and Hampton Court, was brought to Levens.

It is remarkable that the gardens were not redesigned in the 18th century as so many English country-house gardens were. There are also a rose garden, herbaceous borders and a fountain garden.

Above: *English Patchwork from 1708 can be found in the upstairs dressing room at Levens Hall.*

Right: *Levens Hall started life as a defensive towerhouse in the 13th century, but gradually developed into a magnificent Elizabethan country house.*

WALLINGTON HALL

Wallington is one of the finest houses in the north-east. Its exterior, all cool Palladian restraint without the least hint of extravagance, does nothing to prepare the visitor for the florid rococo splendour of the interior, with its richly ornate plasterwork and superb collections of ceramics, needlework and paintings. There is also a unique collection of dolls' houses.

An Immediate Presence

Wallington was built close to the road and therefore without the long drive so beloved of 18th-century country-house builders. It is a solid-looking grey stone building where the visitor is greeted on his or her final approach by four stone griffins' heads on the lawn.

The present building was constructed on the site of a medieval house which, along with its estate, was owned by the Fenwick family, supporters of the Jacobite cause. The Fenwicks sold the estate to Sir William Blackett in 1685, a decade or so before Sir John Fenwick was executed for treason. The house that exists today was first built in 1688, by Sir William's third son (also William) and then substantially altered in the early 18th century. The gardens we see

Below: The 18th-century mansion of Wallington Hall was a hotbed of liberal politics for over 150 years under the ownership of the Trevelyans.

Right: One of a number of beautifully detailed dolls' houses at Wallington Hall.

Opposite: The classical columns in the Dining Room served as a screen to divide the serving area from the dining area.

Below: The four griffins' heads on the lawn at Wallington Hall were brought here from Bishopsgate in the City of London in 1928 by Charles Philips Trevelyan.

now originated in the latter period; they were inspired by the work of Lancelot 'Capability' Brown, who went to school in the Wallington estate village, and were added to by the Trevelyans, later owners.

Extensions and Improvements

In 1728, Wallington passed to William's daughter Elizabeth, who married Sir Walter Calverley. Calverley, who made his money from coal and lead mining, used his fortune to extend and improve the house, adding the façades and bringing Italian craftsmen to this remote corner of Northumberland to complete the plasterwork and other interiors. The clock tower was completed in 1754 and the bridge over the river in 1755. Calverley also built workers' cottages and planted woodlands, and became an MP.

After Calverley died (at the age of 70, making him the oldest member of the House of Commons), the house passed to his sister's son, the first Sir John Trevelyan. The second Sir John's son, Sir Walter, was a friend of the writer and art critic John Ruskin. Walter roofed over the courtyard and commissioned the beautiful paintings by William Bell Scott depicting scenes from Northumberland history that adorn the Central Hall today; the combination of these pictures with the decoration of the hall in imitation of an Italian courtyard produces a curious mixture of the foreign and the domestic. Ruskin himself painted the wild flowers on one of the pilasters in the courtyard.

The last Trevelyan to own Wallington, Sir Charles Philips Trevelyan, became a socialist and gave Wallington Hall to the National Trust on his death in 1958.

Scotland

With their sheer walls, corbelled towers and massive air of impenetrability, the earliest surviving country houses of Scotland reflect the often harsh environment in which they were planned and built. Many should, strictly speaking, be called castles, but for the fact that in the centuries after they were built they were gradually redesigned and remodelled internally to reflect English and continental fashions. And in the 18th century the classical revolution produced houses in Scotland as elegant as any south of the border.

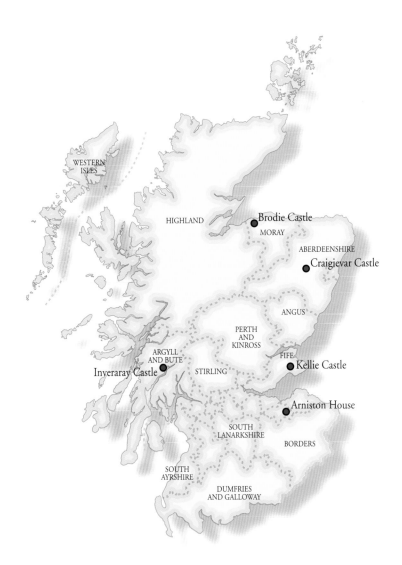

WESTERN
ISLES

HIGHLAND

● Brodie Castle

MORAY

ABERDEENSHIRE

● Craigievar Castle

ANGUS

PERTH
AND
KINROSS

ARGYLL
AND BUTE

FIFE

● Kellie Castle

Inveraray Castle ●

STIRLING

● Arniston House

SOUTH
LANARKSHIRE

BORDERS

SOUTH
AYRSHIRE

DUMFRIES
AND GALLOWAY

ARNISTON HOUSE

Even the terminology associated with grand Scottish houses is very different from that used in England. North of the border people speak not of the parkland or estate surrounding a house, but of the 'policies'. Architecturally, too, Scottish houses are distinctive – older houses tend to be tower houses typically built with corner turrets, rather like French châteaux; and long after English houses ceased to be built in what might best be termed a vaguely fortified style, Scottish houses tended to retain their fortress-like appearance. Nevertheless, the English influence strengthened, particularly after the Act of Union of 1707 and particularly in the lowlands, and as a consequence there exist a number of old tower houses that were rebuilt in the classical 18th-century style. A good example is Arniston, where the Dundas family has lived for over four centuries.

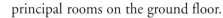
A Palladian Mansion

Situated just a dozen or so miles south of Edinburgh, and a little over a mile from Gorebridge, Arniston was once a typical Scottish tower house, but in 1726 the second Lord Arniston, Robert Dundas, ordered the rebuilding of the old house, which dated from the late 16th century, to create the magnificent Palladian mansion we see today. However, the basement of the old house was retained, together with the two principal rooms on the ground floor.

To carry out the work, which took nearly a quarter of a century to complete, Dundas employed the Adam family, the most fashionable architects of the time. William Adam began the house, which was completed by his son John, the brother of Robert. The two brothers' greatest legacy in Scotland is, of course, Edinburgh's New Town, but they also built a number of Scottish country houses.

Page 187: Inveraray Castle (see pages 203–5) occupies a fantastic position on the shores of Loch Fyne on the western coast of Scotland.

Opposite: Arniston House is a Palladian masterpiece that took nearly a quarter of a century to complete.

Left: The Entrance Hall is a skilful blend of classical, rococo and baroque elements.

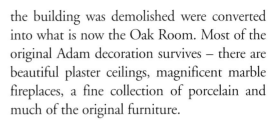

Opposite: Family portraits include works by Scottish masters Sir Henry Raeburn and Allan Ramsay.

Below: Fine Adam plasterwork in the Entrance Hall.

The Dundas Family

Like many great families the Dundas achieved recognition, wealth, power and influence through practice of the law. The family's residence at Arniston began when George Dundas of Dundas, near South Queensferry, married his second wife Katherine Oliphant in the 1560s. Her son, James, born in 1570, could not inherit the Dundas estates because George had an heir by an earlier marriage, so Katherine persuaded her husband to buy Arniston for James. Since that time, each generation has produced its share of MPs, lawyers and judges. By the mid-18th century, the Dundas family was one of the most powerful in Scotland, and the Robert Dundas who rebuilt the house was both Lord Advocate and, finally, Lord President of the Court of Session.

Today, the house contains a number of magnificent portraits of Dundas family members, and many of them by the leading Scottish painters of the day, such as Sir Henry Raeburn and Allan Ramsay.

The two ground-floor rooms of the old tower house that were retained when the rest of the building was demolished were converted into what is now the Oak Room. Most of the original Adam decoration survives – there are beautiful plaster ceilings, magnificent marble fireplaces, a fine collection of porcelain and much of the original furniture.

Victorian Additions

In the 19th century, the architectural firm Wardrop & Reid added a Victorian porch to the front of the house. At the same time the splendid colonnades linking the two pavilions were heightened.

In 1957, dry rot was discovered in the John Adam third of the main block. Two rooms, the Drawing Room and the Dining Room, were almost completely stripped, all the contents being removed so that builders could take the fabric back to the brickwork and beyond in a massive programme of restoration begun in the early 1990s. Both rooms have now been restored.

The Entrance Hall, designed by Adam, still has its original plasterwork. This was carried out by Joseph Enzer and it is a wonderful mass of ribbons, fruit and flowers.

The hall, a skilful blend of classical, rococo and baroque elements, rises to two stories to create a striking impression of grandeur – a perception enhanced by the use of Corinthian pillars to support the ceiling.

The Drawing Room ceiling is a wonderful mass of birds in foliage, and the Dining Room has an elegant coved ceiling with a delicate leafy frieze and a marble fireplace brought here when the Dundas' house in Adam Square, Edinburgh, was demolished. The Victorian Library on the ground floor, installed in the 1860s, has an interesting fireplace in the Flemish style.

The Adam Library, situated at the very top of the house, still has its original stucco work and even the 18th-century glass in the doors of the bookcases.

KELLIE CASTLE

There are records of Kellie as far back as 1150, but the buildings we see today date largely from the 16th and 17th centuries. The castle was owned in the 12th century by an illegitimate son of William the Lion, by the Siward family from 1266 and by the Oliphant family from 1360 until 1613, when it was bought by a childhood friend of James VI, Sir Thomas Erskine. At the time Erskine bought the house, King James also granted him a peerage: he became Viscount Fenton and first Earl Kellie, and, in keeping with his newfound dignity, began to enlarge the castle.

An Estate in Decline

Later Kellies were to support the Jacobite cause, but they were relatively leniently punished after its failure and avoided losing their estates, which was the punishment for most of the old Scottish aristocracy. However, by 1768 mounting debts forced the sixth earl to sell off much of the estate and the seventh earl, who died at Kellie in 1797, was the last of the line. As he had died childless, the house passed to a distant cousin who was also to die without an heir.

By the early 19th century, the title had passed through a series of distant relations to the Earl of Mar, who became the 11th Earl of Kellie. But Mar did not live at Kellie and the house declined; its contents were sold and dereliction became a serious threat, with the Great Hall being used as a barn at the lowest point in its fortunes in the 1860s.

Rescue came in the form of James Lorimer, a law professor from Edinburgh, who took a long lease on Kellie in 1876. The Lorimers were to remain in possession until 1948 when, at last, they were able to buy the castle. When Mary Lorimer died in 1970 the house was presented to the National Trust for Scotland.

Upstairs, Downstairs

Three miles north of Pittenweem in Fife, Kellie Castle is a T-shaped house with three towers; like so many Scottish houses, it began as a simple tower house. The foundations of the first house still exist, and on them was built the 14th-century tower house which still forms the core of the present house. This is now known as the north tower, and it has just one room on each of its five storeys, with a staircase in the south-west corner to connect them.

The bottom two stories would originally have been used for storage and servants' quarters, with the upper storeys kept exclusively for the earl and his family – a complete reversal of the system which prevailed in later, less war-like times when servants were moved to the top of country houses.

Expansion

By the early 17th century, when Thomas Erskine took possession, the simple tower at Kellie must have seemed primitive, so the present east tower was built. Curiously, there is nothing to suggest that the two towers were linked at that time. The second tower, also of five stories, is L-shaped, with the staircase contained in an extension. This stair extends only up to the fourth floor, however; to reach the fifth floor the staircase – now smaller – is corbelled out beyond the main wall.

At the end of the 16th century, the third and final tower – the south tower – was added, and the current block that connects all three towers was constructed.

Despite decades of neglect in the 19th century, much of the interior fabric of the castle survives: there are superb plaster ceilings in a number of rooms, for example, and beautiful painted panelling.

From Bottom to Top

A tour of the house begins at the Lower Hall, or the Crypt, as it is usually known. This is situated on the ground floor along with the wine cellar (now used as a shop), kitchen, store room and pantry. All these rooms have the same beautifully constructed early stone-vaulted ceilings.

From the Crypt we reach the wide stairs and the first floor past a painting (entitled *Any Port in a Storm*) by John Lorimer and an oak table designed by Sir Robert Lorimer. The Great Hall comes next, with its beautiful fireplaces, 17th-century panelling and plasterwork. There are more paintings by members of the

Left: Kellie Castle started out as a tower house, but was greatly extended over succeeding centuries. The house was lucky to survive a serious period of neglect in the 1860s.

Below: Many decorative features, including plasterwork and painted ceilings, survived as a result of intervention by the Lorimer family.

Lorimer family, including a self-portrait by John. The hall leads to the original hall (now the Chapel), which is situated in the oldest part of the house – the late 14th-century north tower. Next comes the Dining Room (formerly the Drawing Room), with its 64 beautifully painted panels, each showing a medieval romance scene. The room also contains a delightful 15th-century stone carving of the Madonna and Child, as well as a 17th-century oak table and a collection of 18th-century china.

An ancient staircase leads up to the Vine Room with its old pine panelling, beautiful plasterwork and marble fireplace, and then on to the Earl's Room, with its gorgeous plaster ceiling and the coat of arms of the third Earl of Kellie. The Professor's Room is devoted to James Lorimer memorabilia.

In the Lorimer Room in the south tower there is a collection of furniture all designed by Sir Robert Lorimer. At the top of the south tower a Victorian nursery has been created; to get to it you have to go up the wonderful little staircase that rises in corbelled masonry on the edge of the main tower.

When you have seen everything in the castle, it is worth taking a few minutes to look at the walled garden, which was created in the 1940s.

Opposite: *The beautiful walled garden was created as recently as the 1940s.*

Below: *Above the fireplace in the Great Hall is a charming and colourful mural, dated 1892, by Phoebe Anna Traquair.*

CRAIGIEVAR CASTLE

Tourists flock to Scotland to see remote and beautiful castles – indeed, like Wales, Scotland is often thought of entirely in terms of castles and dramatic landscapes. Yet, even with its wealth of early fortified buildings one or two still stand out. Among the most interesting is without question Craigievar, perched on its hillside above the Corse Burn about 3 miles from Alford in Strathdon.

A Merchant's House

What makes the house so special is that it was not a grand aristocratic house but the house of a prosperous merchant, plus it retains almost all its original features. The castle, which took more than a decade to build – from 1600 to 1610 – is L-shaped and rises to seven storeys.

William Forbes, who built Craigievar, was an Aberdeen merchant who made his fortune importing timber from the Baltic – hence his nickname 'Danzig Willie'. Forbes was so successful that King Charles I recognized his achievement by knighting his eldest son (also William) in 1630.

Five generations later another William married the daughter of Lord Sempill, and in 1884 their grandson became the 17th Lord Sempill. The main family home then became Fintray, and Craigievar was used only occasionally – a blessing, because this preserved it unmodernized and unspoiled. The National Trust for Scotland took over the castle in 1963.

A Typical Castle

The style is typical of Scottish castle-building of this period, with plain lower walls, decorative upper levels and a single entrance in the massive square tower. Part of the curtain wall of an earlier enclosed courtyard house survives; the wall is certainly older than the present house, but nothing else of that older structure survives.

The entrance brings the visitor immediately into a series of three vaulted cellars. From here a staircase leads to the Hall, with its superb decorated plaster ceiling. Wherever you look there is a plasterwork riot of foliage, heraldic imagery and biblical characters, intricately woven together to create depth and complexity.

At the east end an original timber partition rises to a splendid and very beautiful Minstrels' Gallery. Here you can see the Forbes family motto carved on an oak roundel and dated 1668: 'Doe not waken sleeping dogs.' This was clearly the most important room in the house in earlier times.

Nearby is the Ladies' Withdrawing Room (women traditionally left the men to their conversation when the meal had been eaten), with a plaster ceiling that includes a portrait of Queen Margaret. The Prophet's Room, which is in the main tower of the house, gets its name from the practice of allowing itinerant preachers their bed and board.

Sleeping Quarters

Two ancient turnpike stairs lead to the next floor. Much of the potential space is taken up with the ceiling vault of the hall below, but we also reach the Tartan Bedroom with its Victorian panelling and wonderful portrait of Danzig Willie and his brother Patrick Forbes.

Rising again to the third floor, we reach the Queen's Bedroom, named (according to one story) because Mary, Queen of Scots stayed here or (according to another) because Queen Mary, wife of George V, washed her hands here. This room had the castle's first flushing lavatory, which may well have been installed

Opposite: *A riot of intricate plasterwork is one of the great features of Craigievar Castle.*

Below: *The Queen's Bedroom has splendid portraits of Sir William Forbes and his wife, Lady Sarah.*

in preparation for a visit by Queen Victoria, famously an admirer of this invention.

The beds are 18th-century, the panelling Victorian; there are two Chippendale chairs and portraits by Sir Henry Raeburn, in his day Scotland's greatest portrait painter. One is of the 18th-century Sir William Forbes and his wife, Lady Sarah. Lady Sarah's dressing room nearby has more portraits, including a slightly later one of Sir John and Lady Charlotte Forbes.

On the fourth floor there are the Tank Room (so called because the castle's first water tanks were installed here), a nursery, the Blue Room (a bedroom) and a small dressing room.

Higher still we climb to the fifth floor and the servants' rooms – one of which contains two rare box beds made in the early part of the 19th century. The Long Room may have been used as a picture gallery when the house was first built. A staircase leads to the open platform on top of the square tower, from which there are views down into the remains of the courtyard house and out across the surrounding countryside

BRODIE CASTLE

Romantic and unmistakably Scottish, Brodie Castle, just a few miles from Forres in Morayshire, is a fortified tower house dating back to the mid-16th century, and although it has been added to at different times it would still be familiar to the men who built it more than four centuries ago. Completed in 1567, the castle was the work of the 12th Brodie of Brodie, Alexander, and, like many early Scottish castles, it is built on a Z-plan. It has a central rectangular keep with two towers on diagonally opposite corners. In the 17th century, an extension on the west side of the castle was completed and, in the 19th century, William, the 22nd Brodie of Brodie, commissioned William Burn to build a further extension on the eastern side.

A Strong Lineage

The Brodies are one of Scotland's oldest families: records mention a Brodie of Brodie in the 12th century, and it is believed that they were given their lands by Malcolm IV in about 1160 for services to the crown.

By the 17th century, the Brodies had fallen out with the Stuart monarchy and the castle was partly burned during the religious conflicts of that century after a Brodie signed the Covenant which sought to preserve Presbyterianism in Scotland and to remove royal interference in religious matters. During the 19th century, Brodies served in the British army, became part of the Establishment and restored their fortunes. In the 20th century, the 24th Brodie of Brodie became a world authority on daffodils.

Eight hundred years of Brodies at Brodie Castle came to an end in 2003 with the death of the last direct male descendant, Ninian. A number of years before Ninian's death the castle had passed into the care of the National Trust for Scotland.

Above: *The comfortable sofas remind us that until recently Brodie was the home of one of Scotland's oldest families.*

Opposite: *Brodie Castle is a fine 16th-century Z-plan tower house.*

Below: *The Dining Room is rich in ornate plasterwork and portraits.*

Inside and Out

Some of the rooms today seem a little heavy on the soft furnishings, but there is a great deal of early panelling and plasterwork too, as well as magnificent collections of Chinese, English and continental porcelain. The furniture is predominantly 18th-century French and there is an excellent collection of Scottish watercolours. Other paintings include works by 17th-century Dutch masters.

The policies at Brodie extend to 175 acres and have been restored to their 18th-century appearance. There is a radiating avenue of trees, an ornamental canal and a wilderness area. The daffodil collection is a reminder of the lifelong passion of the 24th Brodie of Brodie.

INVERARAY CASTLE

Inveraray is a mid-18th-century castle that echoes the design of genuine medieval Scottish fortresses but is, in fact, a comfortable house with no real pretensions to military purpose. It was built at the instigation of the third Earl of Islay when he succeeded to the title of Duke of Argyll in 1743.

A Dedicated Follower of Fashion

A much older, largely 15th-century fortified tower once stood on the site: it must have seemed dreadfully old-fashioned and uncomfortable to the duke, who was an enthusiastic follower of fashion and determined that he should have a residence in keeping with his modern views. He called in a London architect, Roger Morris, to oversee the building of his new house; Morris worked under the more famous William Adam, who, in turn, used a design said to

Below: The fortifications of Inveraray Castle, which is built from blue schist stone, are purely cosmetic.

Below: *High windows illuminate the huge space of the Armoury Hall.*

have come from the architect and playwright Sir John Vanbrugh, best known for his work at Blenheim Palace in Oxfordshire.

Inveraray was not finally completed until the 1780s, when the finishing touches were put to the interior decoration for the fifth Duke of Argyll. The interiors alone had taken almost 20 years to complete, and their sumptuousness comes as something of a contrast to the rather austere blue schist stone from which the walls are built.

High windows allow the light to fall spectacularly on the huge space of the Armoury Hall, which rises to more than 60 feet. Displays of armour in country houses are less popular now, but once were a primary attraction; the collection here dates back to 1783 and includes 16th-century pole arms, 18th-century broadswords and early muskets.

French Influences

Next comes the Tapestry Drawing Room – a room that reflects the strong influence of French taste in Scotland in the late 18th century. The room still contains the Beauvais tapestries, known as *Pastorales draperies bleues et arabesques*, commissioned for the house by the fifth Duke of Argyll in 1785, and the splendid architectural decoration and fine plasterwork dates back to the 1780s.

The Victorian Room is best known for the beautiful maplewood writing desk, a wedding present to Princess Louise from her mother Queen Victoria. Louise had married the Marquess of Lorne, later ninth Duke of Argyll, in 1871. The MacArthur Room gets its name from the carved state bed that dominates the room, known as the bed of the MacArthurs of Loch Awe. The MacArthur Room also has some splendid Scottish pictures, including a portrait by the 18th-century artist Gavin Hamilton. In a tiny adjoining room there is a permanent display of photographs relating to the Argylls and their ancestral home.

The Clan Campbell

The Clan Room has a series of changing exhibits, most of which relate to the Clan Campbell (the dukes of Argyll are also head of the Clan Campbell). A genealogical tree illustrates the many branches of the clan and there is a collection of drums from Scottish regiments.

The Saloon, dating from the time of the fifth duke, was designed for everyday living – reading, breakfasting and listening to music. Among the portraits here are a Pompeo Batoni – known as a swagger portrait from its flamboyance – of the eighth Duke of Hamilton and a Gainsborough of

Field Marshal Henry Seymour-Conway, the son-in-law of the fourth Duke of Argyll.

In 1780, Robert Mylne designed the magnificent Dining Room. The overall impression is of elaborate yet delicate decoration, largely the result of the ornamental painting. The beautiful cornice and frieze plasterwork was carried out by John Clayton, a Scotsman, while John Papwith made the ceiling decorations in London before shipping them up to Inveraray. The Dining Room also has wonderful 18th-century ormolu-mounted sideboards, as well as a magnificent late-Georgian Waterford crystal chandelier and a dining table made in 1800 by the Lancaster firm of Gillows.

The chairs are unusual in that they still have their Beauvais tapestry upholstery, but are not French at all: they were made by two Edinburgh carpenters who had been given a French original and told to copy it.

Left: Beauvais tapestries and 1780s plasterwork adorn the Tapestry Drawing Room.

Wales

Like Scotland, Wales was dominated in the medieval period by castle-building, with the erection of many Norman fortresses designed to keep the local population in check. But away from these stern echoes of the past, there are remarkable country houses from a number of periods, such as Tredegar House, the home of one of Wales's most ancient families for almost 500 years, or Bodrhyddan Hall, one of the most romantically situated buildings in Britain.

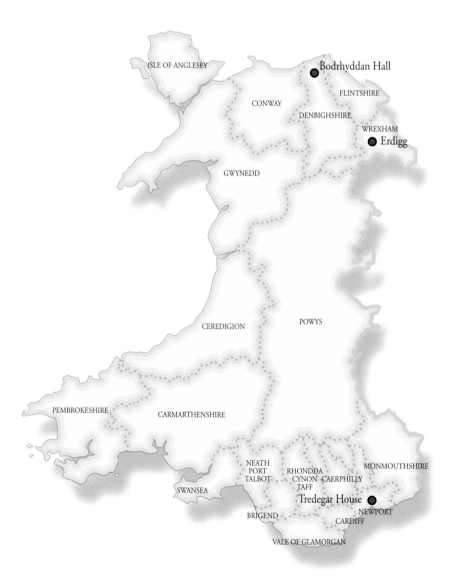

BODRHYDDAN HALL

If it is rare for the same family to retain the same house in England for many centuries, such continuity is even rarer in Wales. One such family, whose Grade I Listed house, Bodrhyddan Hall, deserves to be much better known, is the Conwy family (now Rowley-Conwy). The Conwys have lived at this romantically situated property at the northern end of the Vale of Clwyd for more than 500 years.

Below: *The grounds at Bodrhyddan Hall include an ice-house, a parterre and this beautiful woodland garden.*

Previous page: *One of several elaborate doorways to be found at Tredegar House, near Newport, Gwent.*

Fifteenth-Century Origins

There has been a house on the site for at least 700 years but a much older building probably existed on the site before that. No trace of this original, presumably timber, structure remains. Also, no one quite knows what the name means – the best guess appears to be that Bodrhyddan may derive from something that meant 'the manor house of Rhuddlan'.

The present red-brick house is a remodelling of a 15th-century stone original, and much of the fabric of the early house survives under later work. The 15th-century house was almost certainly built by Sir Richard Conwy and at least one part of it can still be seen: the present cellar door is the original entrance to the semi-fortified Welsh farmhouse, of which the 4-foot-thick outer walls are now the walls of the Great Hall on the ground floor and the Drawing Room inside the house. Fifteenth-century stone floors can also be seen in the Gun Room

and Stone House. When the house was being repaired the original grey stone walls of the Tudor house were discovered here encased in later brick. There is a well in the grounds – St Mary's Well – and above it a delightful octagonal stone well house bearing the date 1612.

Remodelling the Past

Sir Henry Conwy, who was created a baronet by Charles II at the Restoration, drew up plans for the rebuilding of Bodrhyddan, but it was his son, Sir John, who saw the work completed. In essence the house we see today is 17th century, but with major additions completed in the 1870s under the supervision of architect William Eden Nesfield. Nesfield moved the main entrance from the original south-facing range to the west, enabling the creation of an imposing mile-long drive from the village rather than the old short path connecting the house with the road. Nesfield also redesigned the west front in a vaguely Queen Anne style.

On seeing the new work, the celebrated Victorian diarist Augustus Hare commented that 'Bodrhyddan has been changed, restored they call it. Although well done in

Below: *Bodrhyddan Hall dominates the Vale of Clwyd and has been home to the Conwy family for more than 500 years.*

Below: *The fine collection of militaria includes armour that may well have been worn at the Battle of Bosworth in 1485.*

its way, the centuries old charm of the house has quite gone.' The south front of the house is perhaps the most appealing today, with its unusual architectural mix: a centre section built in 1696 in the genuine late 17th-century style but with Queen Anne Revival work on either side.

William Andrews Nesfield, the father of William Eden Nesfield, designed the parterre. William Andrews was a very well-known landscape gardener who redesigned Green Park and had a hand in the layout of Kew Gardens.

Wealthy Women

With the marriage of a daughter and no surviving Conwy sons, in 1778 the house passed to William Shipley, the Dean of St Asaph. In about 1790, he built the Dean's Dining Room – now filled with family

portraits – onto the eastern end of the house.

Before the passing of the Married Women's Property Act in the late Victorian era, on a woman's marriage the whole of her property – with the exception of her wedding ring – passed to her husband; however, it was not unusual for the bride's surname to be incorporated with that of her husband where she brought substantial property to the marriage. Hence, for about 50 years the family name was Shipley-Conwy; and the name underwent a further similar amendment when the present Lord Langford's great-great-grandmother, Charlotte Shipley-Conwy, married Colonel Richard Rowley: hence the present family name of Rowley-Conwy.

In 1953, the then owner, Lord Langford, opened the house and the gardens to the public and the house now has a licence enabling couples to marry here.

Antiquities from England, Egypt and Spain
Internally the house has much to recommend it. The Front Hall displays swords and other militaria used by members of the family and there is some good early armour, including a late 15th-century whole suit which may have been worn at the Battle of Bosworth. The 19th-century passion for Egyptian antiquities brought a superb 3,000-year-old mummy to Bodrhyddan Hall; it is still there today, in the Egyptian Room.

In the Great Hall hang two fine 17th-century portraits, of William Conwy and his wife Luce; a 15th-century table; a 17th-century Chinese tea chest and a beautiful inlaid Dutch longcase clock from about 1700.

The beautiful chimneypieces in the Drawing Room contain panels said to come from a ship of the Spanish Armada wrecked off the coast of Anglesey. They are decorated with biblical scenes. The Drawing Room also contains a Carlton House writing table, a magnificent piece of 18th-century work.

The 8 acres of garden are beautifully planned and kept, and include picnic areas as well as a woodland garden, a walled kitchen garden, an ice house and a beautiful formal parterre. Archaeologists believe that the area known as The Dingle was the site of the medieval fishponds.

Left: *A crossbow, shield and helmets are just part of the vast collection of armoury held at Bodrhyddan Hall.*

Below: *An excellent 17th-century portrait of Luce Conwy hangs in the Great Hall.*

ERDDIG

Erddig is unique among country houses for reasons that have little to do with the building itself. Successive owners of this beautiful old house were unusual in that they treated their servants almost as members of the family, even to the extent of having many of their portraits painted – and that at a time when portrait-painting was a very expensive business indeed.

Below: *The red-brick house of Erddig was where generations of the Yorke family lived, reluctant to make changes.*

Its Own Community

Erddig is also unusual in having preserved many of the functional buildings in which its small army of servants lived and worked: outbuildings little changed in more than a century include a sawmill, smithy, bakehouse, coachhouse, kitchen, laundry and stables.

Inside, much of the house is equally remarkable because successive generations of the Yorke family were reluctant to change or to respond to new fashions. The result is a wonderful legacy; a legacy which shows, uniquely, how a country house like Erddig would have been an almost self-sustaining community with furniture and house repairs, as well as the growing and preparation of

food, all carried out on site.

Erddig also, uniquely, still has the family's collection of carriages, as well as splendid porcelain, magnificent furniture, rare books, sculpture, tapestries and paintings – and a fine state bed dating from the late 17th century with Chinese hangings and a canopy suspended on chains from the ceiling.

A Prominent Position

Erddig was completed in 1687 in a prominent position above the River Clywedog in Denbighshire. It had been commissioned by the newly appointed high sheriff, Joshua Edisbury. The house he built is remarkably plain from the outside, with two floors above a lower ground floor for the servants.

Like many other members of the rising middle class, Joshua Edisbury allowed his sense of his own importance to get the better of him and spent too much on the house and on living in a grand manner. The result was that by the 1690s he was a virtual bankrupt, and much of the furniture had to be sold to

Below: The tapestries of Erddig's Tapestry Room were woven at the Soho factory in 1720, and the furniture dates from the same period.

Below: The family's carts and carriages are still stored and on display in the house's outbuildings.

pay his debts. Edisbury turned to his friend Elihu Yale – a great benefactor of the American university of the same name – and then to his brother for help, but little could be done. Both Edisbury brothers died in poverty in London and Erddig was let.

In 1716, the house was bought by John Meller, a lawyer; the new owner filled it with fine furniture and pictures, most of which are still there. In 1733, the unmarried Meller died, leaving the house to his nephew Simon Yorke. The Yorkes were to remain at

Erddig until the house was handed over to the National Trust in the 1970s.

Acknowledging the Staff

Simon Yorke's son Philip inherited the house aged 23 in 1766, and it was at about this time that the servants at Erddig began to be recorded. Perhaps the most remarkable of all was Betty Radcliffe, Yorke's mother's maid. Betty made the series of extraordinary mother-of-pearl and glass models that can still be seen in the Gallery today. They include

'The Ruins of the Temple of the Sun at Palmyra' and 'The Chinese Pagoda'. The Dining Room has several good family portraits, including a fine example by Thomas Gainsborough of the first Philip Yorke.

The architect James Wyatt refaced the west front and a state bedroom was created on the first floor.

Philip I, who was twice married and had a total of 13 children, belonged to the endearing tradition of eccentric landowners: he became an MP although he loathed politics, rarely attended the House of Commons and never made a speech there!

The second Simon Yorke (Simon II) inherited Erddig in 1804; apart from enlarging the Dining Room and decorating it in the then fashionable Regency style, he did little to change the house. He introduced the strange blue glass bottle fire extinguishers that can still be seen around the house (like many of the Yorkes, he had a morbid fear of fires), and when photography came in he began to commission photographs of the servants

Left: The Chinese Room reflects the passion for all things Oriental that swept the country in the 18th century. Philip Yorke I transformed this room by covering the walls with a Chinese wallpaper that illustrated various lifestyles.

Right: Detail of the decorative gesso gilt work on the state bed in the State bedroom at Erddig

instead of the earlier painted portraits.

Simon's son, Philip II, was married twice, the second time to a passionate cyclist.

The Yorke Recluse

The Simon Yorke who inherited in 1922, became a recluse. He refused offers of help from the Coal Board, whose mining activity was damaging the structure of the house, and cut himself off from the world, refusing to use the post or have electricity installed in the house. In fact, electricity was not installed until the 1970s, and even then the National Trust kept electrical lighting to the minimum in order to preserve the atmosphere.

When Simon died in 1966, his brother Philip inherited and began the long task of repairing the dilapidated house – but he kept together the remarkable collections of pictures, furniture and other artefacts gathered by so many generations of the family. In 1973, the house was presented to the National Trust.

The gardens at Erddig are as fascinating as the house, with pleached limes marking the demolished 18th-century boundary walls, a formal 18th-century garden planned round a canal, a yew walk, a Victorian parterre and a curious waterfall known as the Cup and Saucer. The gardens are also home to the national collections of dozens of varieties of ivy, and there are vegetable, fruit and herb gardens.

The Yorke Local

Local people still speak delightedly of the last of the Yorkes, who took part in the everyday life of the local community and amused everyone with his elaborate alarm system for the house – a long piece of string running from room to room with old tin cans attached at regular intervals. If a burglar entered the house at night and tripped on the string, the rattle of the cans would be sure to wake the inhabitants.

TREDEGAR HOUSE

One of Wales's most ancient families, the Morgans, lived at Tredegar House for almost 500 years: the first Morgan was recorded here as early as 1402 and the last left in 1951. The fine house we see today dates from the Restoration period, but the earliest remains are late 15th century. They were part of a house built by the Morgans, a family who had thrived as a result of supporting the succession to the English throne of the Welshman Henry Tudor. He became Henry VII and the Morgan family was rewarded for their loyalty with land and titles.

Built to Impress

It was not until the 1660s that the Morgans decided they needed a far more impressive house and set about replacing the old stone mansion with a red-brick house, at least partly designed to show the local people that the Morgans were a family to be reckoned with. Apart from the fact that their new house was enormous, brick was then a rare and expensive commodity, particularly in South Wales.

The Morgans' estate here at Tredegar originally extended to more than 1,000 acres but dwindled over the centuries to its present 90 acres. What remains is delightful, however, and includes a beautiful orangery at the back of the house (completed in the early 1700s) and a fine stable block.

The present house incorporates what was probably the south-west wing of the original late medieval house, but none of the contents we see today survived the impact of

Below: *The 90-acre estate at Tredegar includes the splendid early 18th-century orangery.*

Right: The brickwork and elaborate doorways were designed to impress guests.

Below: Fine furniture fills the rooms, but very few pieces are original to the house.

death duties and the mismanagement that plagued the house in the early part of the 20th century. When the last Morgan left in 1951, the house was virtually stripped; it was then used as a school for several decades before being bought and restored by the local council in the 1970s, fortunately escaping the fate of demolition that befell so many early houses in the 1960s.

Bringing Back to Life

The assiduous efforts of the restorers – Newport City Council – and those concerned with running the house resulted in the recovery of the Tredegar Salt, a rare silver salt-cellar inscribed with the Morgan crest; recently bought at auction, it has been restored to the Dining Room. Much of the Morgan china has also been returned to the house along with some furniture and paintings. However, while the original contents are limited, the restoration of the

interior fabric of the house is occasionally dazzling – the restorers have brought the Gilt Room back to life, for example, with its wonderful fireplace and ornate decoration, and the Brown Room has some fine early woodcarvings.

Inigo Jones' Influence

Arguably, however, the chief focus of interest is the outside of the house, for though we do not know the name of the architect the style of the building bears all the hallmarks of Inigo Jones, and whoever built it was undoubtedly influenced by the ideas of that first great English classical architect.

The history of the Morgan family reveals a series of dignified local and national politicians, but also a string of delightful eccentrics, including Catharine Morgan who, convinced she was a bird, went about the estate building nests big enough for her to sit in. The family also produced a pirate (Sir Henry Morgan) and Viscount Evan, who kept numerous exotic animals, including a parrot that swore continually and a kangaroo that was an expert boxer.

Above: The Gilt Room, with its superb fireplace, has been beautifully restored.

Ireland

It is perhaps surprising how many splendid country houses in Ireland have survived the troubled history of one of the most beautiful countries in Europe. Tucked away in remote valleys or out on windswept coasts there are architectural gems from many periods – Bantry House, for example, with its unsurpassed views out over the Atlantic, or Palladian Strokestown Park House or Castle Coole, arguably the masterpiece of the great 18th-century architect James Wyatt.

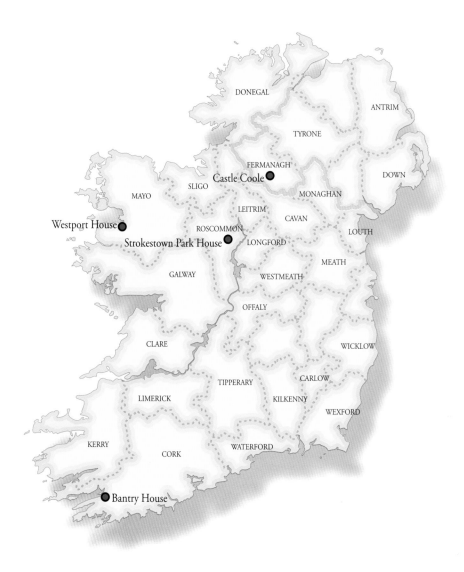

BANTRY HOUSE

Bantry House is rare and special for a number of reasons. First, it has been in the same family since the 18th century; second, it retains most of its original contents – very rare, given the troubled history of Ireland; and last, but by no means least, it was the first house in Ireland to open its doors to the public.

Right: *Reworked and remodelled over a century and more, Bantry House was the first Irish estate to open its doors to the public.*

Previous page: *Bantry House overlooks Bantry Bay in County Cork on the south coast of Ireland.*

A House Full of History

The house has been involved in some of the most momentous events of Irish history. During the terrible famine years of the 1840s, for example, the house and estate provided work for many of the destitute, who helped build the seemingly endless estate wall; and during the Irish Civil War that began in 1922, parts of the house were used as a hospital for the injured on both sides of the conflict.

The history of the house begins in the mid-18th century when the White family, who had lived in Ireland since the 17th century, when they had been part of the English settlement, moved from Whiddy Island in Bantry Bay to the mainland on the south side of the bay. Here they found a five-bay, three-storey house that had been built in the 1720s. Using this house as a core, the family added and embellished it to create the present Bantry House.

Two generations later, Richard White allowed government troops to use Bantry House during the French invasion crisis of 1796 and, despite the fact that the invasion never materialized, was created Baron Bantry in recognition of his services. By 1816 he had been elevated to the peerage as the Earl of Bantry. Richard White had a great love of herons, which he used to watch flying to and from the estate, and had a heron incorporated into the family crest.

Viscount Berehaven's Collections

Additions, improvements and reworkings seem to have been almost constant at Bantry

for the next century and more. A two-storey wing six bays long was built to look out over Bantry Bay in 1820. It was to this newly enlarged house that Richard, Viscount Berehaven (second Earl of Bantry) brought the vast collection of art, furniture, tapestries and other objets d'art he had amassed during numerous trips to Europe between 1820 and 1840. Finding space for his collections insufficient, the viscount built another extension to the rear of the original house. He also added the red-brick pilasters with Coade-stone Corinthian capitals to break up areas of grey stucco, and added a parapet with a balustrade.

Four rooms are of particular interest: the lofty Entrance Hall and staircase; the beautiful Rose Drawing Room, with its mainly French furniture; the Gobelin Drawing Room; and the Library.

A House Full of Objects
The house is a wonderful jumble of rare and fascinating objects. In the Entrance Hall, for

STROKESTOWN PARK HOUSE

Strokestown's greatest claim to fame may well be that it was the scene of the assassination of Victorian owner Major Denis McMahon, notorious for chartering unseaworthy 'coffin ships' to carry his evicted tenants to America. Many of the ships sank, and conditions on even those that did make it to America were so dreadful that huge numbers died en route.

Below: Strokestown Park House sits at the end of Ireland's widest main street, which was designed by the second Lord Hartland.

Tragedy and Troubles

The memory of terrible events should not entirely eclipse one's perception of this beautiful house, however, for Strokestown remains one of the great Irish Palladian houses, and its survival is a tribute to the many ordinary Irishmen and -women among the craftspeople who built and maintained it.

It was built in the 18th century by the German architect Richard Cassels, also known as Richard Castle, for Thomas Mahon on land that had been given to the family by the British crown two generations earlier. It stands at the end of Ireland's widest main street on the edge of the small village of Strokestown itself.

Though at first glance it may not be obvious, Strokestown incorporates an earlier tower house, typical of the sort of fortified dwellings common in what was, at the time it would have been built, a troubled country.

How the Anglo-Irish Once Lived

Today it is divided into a central three-storey residential block, a north wing containing a rare galleried kitchen – the gallery allowed the mistress of the house to keep an eye on the servants without getting dirty among them – and a south wing with a beautiful vaulted ceiling (held up by Tuscan columns), that serves as the stable block. The central block and wings are connected by an elegantly curving screen wall decorated with niches and pedimented archways.

The date 1696 is carved over the front door, but the wings were added later, probably in the 1740s. The fireplaces, porch, doors, cornicing and Library date from the early 19th century, but externally the house has retained its original Palladian proportions.

The Staircase Hall retains its original and rather beautiful panelling. The Dining Room has all the look of the Regency period,

with its red damask wallpaper and fine furniture; there is also a wonderful (and vast!) turf bucket in this room, turf being the favoured Irish domestic fuel.

At the back of the house a ballroom with a curving wall was added in the early 19th century; later turned into a library, it still has its Chippendale bookcases and gold wallpaper.

If grand reception rooms dominate the ground floor, upstairs visitors can see from the small bedrooms, fully equipped Victorian nursery and schoolroom how the children of an aristocratic Anglo-Irish family would have lived in the 19th century. There is also a room filled with documents relating to the famine that killed almost two million men, women and children in the 1840s.

The current owner of the house saved it from almost certain demolition when he bought it complete with its contents in 1979.

Below left: A gallery in the kitchen ensured that the mistress of the house could keep an eye on the servants.

Below far left: A view across the formal garden.

Below: Even the phones at Strokestown Park House are original.

WESTPORT HOUSE

Dennis Browne, the present owner of Westport House, is a direct descendant of Grace O'Malley, the 16th-century 'Pirate Queen of Connaught' (legend has it she even gave birth at sea) – a romantic connection that entirely matches the romance of one of the world's most beautifully situated houses.

A Romantic Setting

Westport's wonderful position, on the shores of Clew Bay, looking out across the Atlantic to Clare Island some 15 miles away, was summed up by the author William Thackeray, who visited the house in 1842 and wrote: 'I think it forms an event in one's life to have seen that place, so beautiful is it.'

The Brownes have been at Westport since the house was first built. The first John Browne, an Englishman, arrived in Ireland in 1580. He made his home at a place called The Neale near Kilmaine, and it was his grandson, another John, who married Maud Bourke, the great-grand-daughter of Grace O'Malley, whose family owned the original castle on the site.

The bulk of the present house, completed in the early 1730s, is the work of the German architect Richard Cassels. He was commissioned to remodel the house by another John Browne who later became the first Earl of Altamont. Cassels didn't completely destroy the house he worked on,

Opposite: *Westport House, with its lake and landscaped gardens, is the work of German architect, Richard Cassels.*

Below: *Elaborate Adamesque plasterwork in blue and gold lifts the Dining Room ceiling.*

CASTLE COOLE

Completed in 1798 after a decade of continuous work, Castle Coole is one of Ireland's greatest houses and arguably the masterpiece of the great 18th-century architect James Wyatt. The house, long the home of the Earls of Belmore, stands in unspoiled parkland on the outskirts of Enniskillen in Northern Ireland's County Fermanagh.

Below: *Castle Coole as seen from the wide waters of Lough Erne.*

Unspoiled Surroundings

The house was commissioned by the first Earl of Belmore, who brought in craftsmen and decorators, plasterers and joiners from all over the British Isles and beyond, regardless of the cost. Richard Westmacott created the intricately carved fireplaces; Joseph Rose executed the superb plasterwork.

Castle Coole has one of the best collections of Regency furniture in the British Isles, with furniture, chairs and other items all supplied for the house by the Dublin upholsterer John Preston between 1807 and 1825. Wyatt supplied designs for the furniture for the Hall and Dining Room which was then made by the joiners on site.

Sumptuous Interiors

It was Belmore's son, the second earl, who redecorated and furnished the house in the latest style in the early years of the 19th century. The state rooms are sumptuous, and no visitor should miss the State Bedroom, which is said to have been prepared specially

for a visit by George IV – who, in the event, failed to turn up. Supplied in 1821 by John Preston, the beautifully carved bed is hung with flame-coloured, restored silk and the original lavish gold-coloured trimmings, which are in remarkably good condition.

Just as interesting, indeed perhaps more so from a modern perspective, is the Basement where the servants lived and worked. Running the full length of the house, it has not been used for many years, but the National Trust, which acquired the house in 1951, hopes to conserve these fading interiors and enable greater public access to them.

Dotted here and there about the house and outbuildings are other fascinating items, including an early 19th-century Broadwood piano, a beautifully preserved 19th-century carriage, a Victorian dolls' house, a collection of 18th-century Derby ware and some good, if not spectacular, pictures.

Just as splendid as the inside of Castle Coole is its setting amid 700 landscaped acres, woodland and the nearby shores of Lough Coole. There are peaceful walks to the lough edge, an ice house and stables by Richard Morrison.

Above: The State Bedroom.

PICTURE ACKNOWLEDGEMENTS

All pictures taken by Paul Riddle, except for:

Page 46: National Trust Photographic Library/Nadia Mackenzie
Page 47: National Trust Photographic Library/Michael Allwood-Coppin
Page 48: National Trust Photographic Library
Page 49: National Trust Photographic Library/Derek Croucher
Page 50: National Trust Photographic Library/Rob Matheson
Page 51: Courtesy of Squerryes Court
Page 57: National Trust Photographic Library/Bill Davis
Page 58: National Trust Photographic Library/Stephen Robson
Page 59: National Trust Photographic Library/Bill batten
Page 60: National Trust Photographic Library/Andreas von Einsiedel
Pages 66–9: English Heritage Photographic Library
Page 94: National Trust Photographic Library/Andrew Butler
Page 95–8: National Trust Photographic Library/Andreas von Einsiedel
Page 102: National Trust Photographic Library/Andrew Butler
Page 103: National Trust Photographic Library/Andreas von Einsiedel
Pages 104–105 and back cover: Courtesy of Blenheim Palace
Page 111: National Trust Photographic Library/Vera Collingwood
Page 112: National Trust Photographic Library/Nadia Mackenzie
Page 113: National Trust Photographic Library/David Dixon
Page 114: National Trust Photographic Library/Andreas von Einsiedel
Page 115: National Trust Photographic Library/Nick Meers
Pages 116–17: National Trust Photographic Library/A.F. Kersting
Page 118: National Trust Photographic Library/David Sellman
Page 120: National Trust Photographic Library/David Hunter
Page 147: Chris Coe
Page 148: National Trust Photographic Library/Andreas von Einsiedel
Page 149: National Trust Photographic Library/Roger Hickman
Page 150: National Trust Photographic Library/Nadia Mackenzie
Page 151: National Trust Photographic Library/Andreas von Einsiedel
Page 158: National Trust Photographic Library/Nick Meers
Pages 159–61: National Trust Photographic Library/Andreas von Einsiedel
Page 183: National Trust Photographic Library/Matthew Antrobus
Pages 184 & 185: National Trust Photographic Library/Andreas von Einsiedel
Page 184–5: National Trust Photographic Library/David Tarn
Pages 168–72: Courtesy of Harewood House
Pages 181–2: Courtesy of Levens Hall
Page 212: National Trust Photographic Library/Rupert Truman
Page 213: National Trust Photographic Library/Andreas von Einsiedel
Page 214: National Trust Photographic Library/Rupert Truman
Pages 215 & 216: National Trust Photographic Library/Andreas von Einsiedel
Pages 232–3: National Trust Photographic Library/Matthew Antrobus
Page 233: National Trust Photographic Library/Christopher Hill